ICAS 2023

The Nineteenth International Conference on Autonomic and Autonomous Systems

March 13th - 17th, 2023

Barcelona, Spain

ICAS 2023 Editors

Carsten Behn, Schmalkalden University of Applied Sciences, Germany

Printed from e-media with permission by:

Curran Associates, Inc.
57 Morehouse Lane
Red Hook, NY 12571

Some format issues inherent in the e-media version may also appear in this print version.

Printed with permission by Curran Associates, Inc. (2023)

International Academy, Research, and Industry Association (IARIA)
412 Derby Way
Wilmington, DE 19810

Phone: (408) 893-6407
Fax: (408) 527-6351

petre@iaria.org

Additional copies of this publication are available from:

Curran Associates, Inc.
57 Morehouse Lane
Red Hook, NY 12571 USA
Phone: 845-758-0400
Fax: 845-758-2633
Email: curran@proceedings.com
Web: www.proceedings.com

Table of Contents

ICAS 2023

Foreword

The Nineteenth International Conference on Autonomic and Autonomous Systems (ICAS 2023), held between March 13 – 17, 2023, was a multi-track event covering related topics on theory and practice on systems automation, autonomous systems and autonomic computing.

The main tracks referred to the general concepts of systems automation, and methodologies and techniques for designing, implementing and deploying autonomous systems. The next tracks developed around design and deployment of context-aware networks, services and applications, and the design and management of self-behavioral networks and services. We also considered monitoring, control, and management of autonomous self-aware and context-aware systems and topics dedicated to specific autonomous entities, namely, satellite systems, nomadic code systems, mobile networks, and robots. It has been recognized that modeling (in all forms this activity is known) is the fundamental for autonomous subsystems, as both managed and management entities must communicate and understand each other. Small-scale and large-scale virtualization and model-driven architecture, as well as management challenges in such architectures are considered. Autonomic features and autonomy requires a fundamental theory behind and solid control mechanisms. These topics gave credit to specific advanced practical and theoretical aspects that allow subsystem to expose complex behavior. We aimed to expose specific advancements on theory and tool in supporting advanced autonomous systems. Domain case studies (policy, mobility, survivability, privacy, etc.) and specific technology (wireless, wireline, optical, e-commerce, banking, etc.) case studies were targeted. A special track on mobile environments was indented to cover examples and aspects from mobile systems, networks, codes, and robotics.

Pervasive services and mobile computing are emerging as the next computing paradigm in which infrastructure and services are seamlessly available anywhere, anytime, and in any format. This move to a mobile and pervasive environment raises new opportunities and demands on the underlying systems. In particular, they need to be adaptive, self-adaptive, and context-aware.

Adaptive and self-management context-aware systems are difficult to create, they must be able to understand context information and dynamically change their behavior at runtime according to the context. Context information can include the user location, his preferences, his activities, the environmental conditions and the availability of computing and communication resources. Dynamic reconfiguration of the context-aware systems can generate inconsistencies as well as integrity problems, and combinatorial explosion of possible variants of these systems with a high degree of variability can introduce great complexity.

Traditionally, user interface design is a knowledge-intensive task complying with specific domains, yet being user friendly. Besides operational requirements, design recommendations refer to standards of the application domain or corporate guidelines.

Commonly, there is a set of general user interface guidelines; the challenge is due to a need for cross-team expertise. Required knowledge differs from one application domain to another, and the core knowledge is subject to constant changes and to individual perception and skills.

Passive approaches allow designers to initiate the search for information in a knowledge-database to make accessible the design information for designers during the design process. Active approaches, e.g., constraints and critics, have been also developed and tested. These mechanisms deliver information (critics) or restrict the design space (constraints) actively, according to the rules and guidelines. Active and passive approaches are usually combined to capture a useful user interface design.

We take here the opportunity to warmly thank all the members of the ICAS 2023 Technical Program Committee, as well as the numerous reviewers. The creation of such a high quality conference program would not have been possible without their involvement. We also kindly thank all the authors who dedicated much of their time and efforts to contribute to ICAS 2023. We truly believe that, thanks to all these efforts, the final conference program consisted of top quality contributions.

Also, this event could not have been a reality without the support of many individuals, organizations, and sponsors. We are grateful to the members of the ICAS 2023 organizing committee for their help in handling the logistics and for their work to make this professional meeting a success.

We hope that ICAS 2023 was a successful international forum for the exchange of ideas and results between academia and industry and for the promotion of progress in the fields of autonomic and autonomous systems.

We are convinced that the participants found the event useful and communications very open. We also hope that Barcelona provided a pleasant environment during the conference and everyone saved some time for exploring this beautiful city.

ICAS 2022 Chairs:

ICAS 2023 Steering Committee

Roy Sterritt, Ulster University, UK
Mark J. Balas, Texas A&M University, USA
Karsten Böhm, Fachhochschule Kufstein, Austria
Jacques Malenfant, Sorbonne Université | LIP6 Lab, France
Claudius Stern, biozoom services GmbH - Kassel | FOM University of Applied Sciences – Essen, Germany

ICAS 2023 Publicity Chairs

Sandra Viciano Tudela, Universitat Politecnica de Valencia, Spain
José Miguel Jiménez, Universitat Politecnica de Valencia, Spain

ICAS 2023

Committee

ICAS 2023 Steering Committee
Roy Sterritt, Ulster University, UK
Mark J. Balas, Texas A&M University, USA
Karsten Böhm, Fachhochschule Kufstein, Austria
Jacques Malenfant, Sorbonne Université | LIP6 Lab, France
Claudius Stern, biozoom services GmbH - Kassel | FOM University of Applied Sciences – Essen, Germany

ICAS 2023 Publicity Chairs
Sandra Viciano Tudela, Universitat Politecnica de Valencia, Spain
José Miguel Jiménez, Universitat Politecnica de Valencia, Spain

ICAS 2023 Technical Program Committee

Mubarak Abdu-Aguye, Mohamed bin Zayed University of Artificial Intelligence, UAE
Lounis Adouane, Université de Technologie de Compiègne (UTC), France
Waseem Akram, University of Calabria, Italy
Getachew Alemu, Addis Ababa University, Ethiopia
Alba Amato, Institute for High-Performance Computing and Networking (ICAR), Napoli, Italy
Arash Amini, Lehigh University, USA
Vijayan K. Asari, University of Dayton, USA
Mark Balas, Texas A&MUniversity, USA
Malek Ben Salem, Accenture Labs, USA
Julita Bermejo-Alonso, Universidad Politécnica de Madrid (UPM), Spain
Sylvain Bertrand, ONERA - The French Aerospace Lab - Centre de Palaiseau, France
Navneet Bhalla, University College London, UK
Estela Bicho, University of Minho / Centre Algoritmi / CAR group, Portugal
Karsten Böhm, Fachhochschule Kufstein, Austria
Kamel Bouzgou, Université des sciences et de la technologie Oran USTO-MB, Algeria / Université Paris Saclay - Univ. Evry, France
Estelle Bretagne, University of Picardie Jules Verne / lab MIS (modeling, information and systems), France
Ivan Buzurovic, Harvard University, Boston, USA
Paolo Campegiani, Bit4id, Italy
Alberto Castagna, Trinity College Dublin, Ireland
Wen-Chung Chang, Taipei Tech, Taiwan
Shuo Cheng, Georgia Tech, USA
Marco Claudio Campi, University of Brescia, Italy
Valérie Camps, Paul Sabatier University - IRIT, Toulouse, France
Elisa Capello, Politecnico di Torino and CNR-IEIIT, Italy
Constantin F. Caruntu, "Gheorghe Asachi" Technical University of Iasi, Romania
Samuel Cerqueira Pinto, Magna Advanced Development Center, USA
Meghan Chandarana, NASA Ames Research Center, USA

Juncheng Li, East China Normal University, Shanghai, China
Sen Li, The Hong Kong University of Science and Technology, Hong Kong
Yangmin Li, The Hong Kong Polytechnic University, Hong Kong
Zhan Li, Swansea University, UK
Enjie Liu, University of Bedfordshire, UK
Eric Lucet, CEA | LIST | Interactive Robotics Laboratory, Palaiseau, France
Ren C. Luo, National Taiwan University, Taiwan
Nacer K M'Sirdi, Aix-Marseille Université, France
Jacques Malenfant, Sorbonne Université - CNRS, France
Guilhem Marcillaud, Paul Sabatier University, IRIT, France
Aurelian Marcu, Center for Advance Laser technology CETAL - National Institute for Laser Plasma and Radiation Physics, Romania
Raúl Marín Prades, Jaume-I University, Spain
Philippe Martinet, INRIA Sophia Antipolis, France
Ignacio Martinez-Alpiste, University of the West of Scotland, UK
Rajat Mehrotra, Teradata Inc., Santa Clara,, USA
René Meier, Hochschule Luzern, Switzerland
Oliver Michler, Technical University Dresden, Germany
Sérgio Monteiro, Centro Algoritmi | University of Minho, Portugal
Naghmeh Moradpoor, Edinburgh Napier University, UK
Paulo Moura Oliveira, UTAD University, Vila Real, Portugal
Luca Muratore, Istituto Italiano di Tecnologia, Genova, Italy / The University of Manchester, UK
Taro Nakamura, Chuo University, Japan
Roberto Nardone, University of Reggio Calabria, Italy
Rafael Oliveira Vasconcelos, Federal University of Sergipe (UFS), Brazil
Flavio Oquendo, IRISA - University of South Brittany, France
Luigi Palmieri, Robert Bosch GmbH, Corporate Research, Germany
Eros Pasero, Politecnico di Turin, Italy
Timothy Patten, University of Technology Sydney, Australia
Ling Pei, Shanghai Jiao Tong University, China
Damien Pellier, Université Grenoble Alpes, France
Van-Toan Pham, Vietnam Maritime University, Vietnam / National Taipei University of Technology, Taiwan
Agostino Poggi, DII - University of Parma, Italy
Radu-Emil Precup, Politehnica University of Timisoara, Romania
Leonīds Ribickis, Riga Technical University, Latvia
Douglas Rodrigues, Paulista University - UNIP, Brazil
Oliver Roesler, Vrije Universiteit Brussel, Belgium
Joerg Roth, Nuremberg Institute of Technology, Germany
Loris Roveda, Università della Svizzera italiana (USI), Switzerland
Spandan Roy, International Institute of Information Technology, Hyderabad, India
Fariba Sadri, Imperial College London, UK
Mohammad Safeea, Coimbra University, Portugal / ENSAM, Lille, France
Lakhdar Sais, CNRS | Artois University, Lens, France
Michael A. Saliba, University of Malta, Malta
Ivan Samylovskiy, Lomonosov Moscow University, Russia
Ricardo Sanz, Universidad Politecnica de Madrid, Spain
Jagannathan Sarangapani, Missouri University of Science and Technology, USA

André Schneider de Oliveira, Federal University of Technology - Parana, Brazil
Vesna Sesum-Cavic, TU Wien, Austria
Mahmoud Shafiee, University of Kent, Canterbury, UK
Abdel-Nasser Sharkawy, South Valley University, Qena, Egypt
Inderjeet Singh, University of Texas at Arlington Research Institute (UTARI), USA
Edoardo Sinibaldi, Istituto Italiano di Tecnologia (IIT), Italy
J. Tanner Slagel, NASA Langley Research Center, USA
Mohammad Divband Soorati, University of Southampton, UK
Iderli Souza, Federal University of Pampa, Brazil
Bernd Steinbach, University of Mining and Technology, Freiberg, Germany
Claudius Stern, FOM University of Applied Sciences, Essen, Germany
Roy Sterritt, Ulster University, UK
Yun-Hsuan Su, University of Washington, Seattle, USA
Saied Taheri, Virginia Tech, USA
Omar Tahri, PRISME | INSA Centre Val-de-Loire, France
Brahim Tamadazte, FEMTO-ST Institute / CNRS, France
Maryam Tebyani, University of California, Santa Cruz, USA
Francesco Tedesco, University of Calabria, Italy
Giorgio Terracina, Università della Calabria, Italy
Carlos M. Travieso-González, Institute for Technological Development and Innovation in Communications (IDeTIC) | University of Las Palmas de Gran Canaria (ULPGC), Spain
Xuan-Tung Truong, Le Quy Don Technical University, Vietnam
Eddie Tunstel, Motiv Space Systems Inc. / Motiv Robotics, USA
Paulo Urbano, Universidade de Lisboa, Portugal
Vivek Shankar Varadharajan, École Polytechnique de Montréal, Canada
Ramon Vilanova, School of Engineering - UAB, Spain
Nikolaos (Nikos) Vitzilaios, University of South Carolina, USA
Holger Voos, University of Luxembourg, Luxembourg
Stefanos Vrochidis, Information Technologies Institute | Centre for Research and Technology Hellas, Greece
Wenbin Wan, University of Illinois at Urbana-Champaign, USA
Dingkang Wang, University of Florida, USA
Yin-Tien Wang, Tamkang University, Taipei, Taiwan
Guowu Wei, University of Salford, UK
Luke Wood, University of Hertfordshire, UK
Haiyan Wu, CAS Key Laboratory of Behavioral Science | University of Chinese Academy of Sciences, China
Yuanlong Xie, Huazhong University of Science and Technology, China
Jiajun Xu, Nanjing University of Aeronautics and Astronautics, China
Reuven Yagel, Azrieli - Jerusalem College of Engineering, Israel
Oleg Yakimenko, Naval Postgraduate School, USA
Boling Yang, University of Washington, USA
Chenguang Yang, University of the West of England, Bristol, UK
Lee Jing Yang, Nanyang technological University, Singapore
Linda Yang, University of Portsmouth, UK
Ali Zemouche, Université de Lorraine, France
Haichao Zhang, Horizon Robotics, USA

Vadim Zhmud, Novosibirsk State Technical University, Russia
Huiyu (Joe) Zhou, University of Leicester, UK

Mobile 3D LiDAR-based Object and Change Detection in Production and Operations Management

Taru Hakanen, Paul Kemppi and Petri Tikka
Cognitive Production Industry
VTT Technical Research Centre of Finland
Tampere, Finland
email: taru.hakanen@vtt.fi

Abstract—**As an ongoing robot-related trend, intelligent mobile robots can create an accurate digital three-dimensional (3D) model of the environment using Light Detection And Ranging (LiDAR) scanners. This paper presents a new solution concept, which enables change detection and thus more efficient visual 3D data utilisation in production and operations management. As a result, use cases for mobile, real-time 3D LiDAR-based change detection are identified. In these cases, Autonomous Mobile Robots (AMRs) equipped with LiDARs detect changes automatically while moving around the factory in, e.g., internal logistics tasks. The solution studied may be useful for, e.g., detecting large items left in the wrong places, obstacles on AMRs' routes and blocked fire doors and emergency exits. The as-is 3D model of the factory can also be used as a basis for factory renovation and modernisation and progress monitoring.**

Keywords-Autonomous mobile robot; AMR; LiDAR; object and change detection; real-time

I. INTRODUCTION

Modern factories are full of fixed sensors on production lines and machines, as well as in the building itself. There have been plenty of discussions and actions taken in smart factories in order to unleash the potential of Industry 4.0 and enormous amounts of data [1]. AMRs and digital twins are among central technologies when companies proceed in Industry 4.0 and 5.0 [2][3]. AMRs use LiDAR scanners in mapping their environment, localisation and autonomous navigation [4]-[8]. With 3D LiDARs, an accurate digital reconstruction can be created of the environment where the AMR is moving while conducting, e.g., internal logistics tasks. However, data gathered by LiDARs remain under utilised in factories, and new mobile LiDAR solutions can enable new use cases and benefits for production and operations management.

The aim of this study was to study the way mobile 3D LiDAR-based object and change detection can enhance production and operations management (POM). The study consisted of two tasks: 1) development of a new mobile, real-time 3D LiDAR-based solution concept for object and change detection and related testing in real industrial environments and 2) identification of potential use cases for such solutions within the production and operations management domain. The findings of the study propose new potential use cases for object and change detection in, e.g., production, intra-logistics and security operations. The strengths of the solution are especially related to cases in which rather large visual objects and changes need to be detected. Then, for example, obstacles blocking AMR traffic or emergency exits can be pinpointed real-time leading to prompt reactions and thus ensuring smooth logistics flows and safety.

This paper is organised as follows: Section 1 provides an introduction for the paper. In the Section 2, we provide a theoretical background regarding digital smart factories, AMRs, LiDARs and related applications, as well as methods for object and change detection. Section 3 describes the methodology of the study. Section 4 presents the study results: a) a technical solution concept for object and change detection and testing results in a real industrial environment, and b) potential use cases for the solution. Finally, in the Section 5, conclusions are drawn on the most potential use cases and the ways the solution may enhance POMS in the future.

II. THEORY

A. Intelligent production and operations

Industry 4.0, also known as the Fourth Industrial Revolution, is drastically renewing manufacturing companies' production and operations [2]. Digital technologies make machines more self-sufficient, highly data intensive and able to communicate and even "talk" to one another. Automation and data analytics emerge as major forces to enhance efficiency in operations management [9]. The ultimate aim is to enhance production and operations efficiency and business growth.

Hand in hand with the phenomenon goes the trend of making all businesses smarter and more automated [9]. Manufacturing is in an increasing manner equipped with sensor and autonomous systems. Dull, dirty and dangerous labour involves in an increasing manner robots instead of people. Robotics and digital twins are two out of five central disruptive technologies in the Industry 4.0 and beyond [9]. Robots are more intelligent and autonomous and support automation of production and intra-logistics operations. In addition to robotics, holistically digitalised models of products and factories are developed for smart factories [10]. Industry 5.0 also includes edge computing, digital twins and collaborative robots also encompassing stronger human perspective in terms of critical thinking and decision making [3][9].

Industry 4.0 and 5.0 go hand in hand with the Big Data phenomenon [12], and huge amounts of various data from machines and operations are collected and used nowadays in factories. Data supports rehal-time monitoring and more intelligent decision making concerning, for example, production and inventory management [1][4][12]. Fifth-generation (5G) network enables further advances in data gtransfer, remote monitoring and operation [13].

B. Autonomous mobile robots in smart factory

Traditionally, motives for automation have been cost savings, quality improvements and safety [14]. Use of AMRs is increasing in production and intralogistics operations [5][14]. AMRs are typically equipped with a wide set of sensing technologies providing input data. Laser scanners, 3D cameras, accelerometers, gyroscopes, ultrasound sensors and wheel encoders ensure accurate position and heading data at all times, thus enabling safe autonomous navigation [5][6][15][16]. Although huge amounts of data are often collected with fixed sensors in factories, data that AMRs collect while driving around remains underutilised. We suggest that data collected with laser scanners, 3D LiDARs, could also be used more in production and operations management.

Figure 1. SPOT robot as an example of an AMR.

During the past ten years, the use of 3D LiDARs has grown rapidly. LiDAR stands for Light Detection And Ranging. LiDARs uses light pulses, typically emitted by a laser, to measure distances of its surroundings. LiDARs provide a precise distance point cloud relative to the AMR of its environment, which is then used for Simultaneous Localisation And Mapping (SLAM) and collision avoidance [6]-[8][17]-[19]. As a result, a point cloud consisting of as many as millions of dots is created, and a digital twin of the environment is created (Figure 2). More knowledge is needed on, how point clouds formed by AMR 3D LiDARs could be used to accrue benefits for production and operations management.

Figure 2. Point cloud created with 3D LiDAR scanner.

C. 3D LiDAR applications in various business fields

LiDARs are widely in use in various business fields. In the manufacturing industry, one of the most common applications of LiDARs is for autonomous navigation of AMRs and automated guided vehicles (AGVs) in internal logistics operations [4]-[8]. Accurate, as-built 3D models of industrial sites could be used more in the manufacturing sector [4] for, e.g., site modernisation projects, inspection, safety analysis, simulation and change detection.

In addition to AMRs and AGVs in industrial use, another common application area for LiDARs is transportation. LiDAR data can be collected, e.g., by cars on the ground, by airplanes or drones in the air or by satellites in space [20]. In these cases, LiDAR data is mobile, whereas in some cases, data can also be collected statically, e.g., when modelling a building. In this paper, we concentrate on mobile laser scanning, which is LiDAR mounted on a mobile platform, moving on a factory floor or outdoor at a factory site. Mobile LiDAR scanning is the most common approach for collecting data in transportation applications, since roads and various features of urban environments can be captured with a high level of detail [20]-[22]. Further applications for LiDARs include, e.g., mapping mines [23][24], cities and buildings [25]-[28], forests [29], plants and fields [30] and historical landscapes in archaeological research [31].

D. 3D LiDAR-based object and change detection

LiDAR sensors target the surrounding surfaces with a laser beam and produce range data by measuring the time for the reflected light to return to the receiver. For instance, Ouster OS0-128 LiDAR has a 360°×90° field-of-view and a measuring range from 0.5m up to 100m. These wide angle, high resolution LiDARs provide opportunities not only for localisation, navigation and mapping, but also for detection and monitoring temporal changes.

3D-change-detection tasks aim to find differences in a scene or for particular types of objects using multiple acquisitions of 3D data. 3D LiDARs scan the environment at a high speed (e.g., 20 times per second), and every time, a point cloud consisting of as many as millions of dots is created. For instance, with an angular resolution of 0.2°×0.7° Ouster OS0-128 LiDAR is able to provide up to 2621440 points per second, with a precision of ±1.5–5cm. Point clouds collected at different times are then compared for detecting changes. The changes in the 3D geometry can be further categorised as additions (previously free space is now occupied), subtractions (previously occupied space is now free) or discrepancies, where the apparent change is caused by sensor noise or other sources of error [32]. In addition to data differentiation, change detection may also include identification of changes for meaningful objects. For instance, monitoring of an on-street car park included 1) vehicle detection, 2) classification in terms of defined categories of vehicles and 3) change detection in terms of whether a car had changed from a certain spot in order to estimate parking duration [33].

3D object detection can be divided into three kinds of methodologies: 1) fusion-based approaches, combining RGB images and 3D point cloud data, 2) two-dimensional (2D) detection-driven methods, based on 2D bounding boxes defined from RGB images and 3) point-cloud-based methods, exploring features and topology of points to detect 3D objects [34]. In this paper, we concentrate on the latter one, point-cloud-based methods. 3D LiDARs can create a very accurate digital 3D model and map of the environment, even in environments where there are people [35]. When a mobile robot gathers 3D LiDAR data, object steric size and location information are included. Another benefit of LiDARs is that they are insensitive to natural light, which makes them a potential sensor for 3D detection in environments with varying or poor light conditions. In many cases, methods based on RGB images and image recognition are feasible for object and change detection [36]. However, while comparing LiDAR-based methods with the 2D object detection, LiDAR-based methods can provide new potential applications for production and operations management.

One state-of-the-art point-cloud-based object and change detection method is a method called PointPillars, in which point cloud data is combined with voxel-based feature extraction [37]. First, it organises raw point clouds as pillars (voxels) and then uses PointNet to learn the representation of point clouds. Finally, a standard 2D convolutional is used to enable efficient real-time detection. This method has been used, e.g., in autonomous vehicles for pedestrian and cyclist detection [38][39].

E. Literature synthesis, research gap and research question

3D LiDARs have been traditionally used for mapping the environment, robot localisation and autonomous navigation [4]-[8]. In recent years, the advances in LiDAR technology have improved their range, accuracy and resolution. At the same time, laser scanners' prices have gone down significantly in relation to their improved capabilities. Object detection, classification and 3D change detection can be done in a more detailed level than before and new use cases can be identified in factories. Still, within the production and operations management domain, there is scarcity of research concerning future mobile 3D LiDAR-based concepts, solutions and potential use cases that can emerge in this context. Object and change detection done with 3D LiDARs may offer new benefits for the industry. It is one way in which mobile LiDAR data collected by AMR on site can be taken into more efficient use in so-called smart factories. Thus, the main research question of this paper is the following: *"How can mobile 3D LiDAR-based object and change detection enhance production and operations management in smart factories?"*

III. METHODOLOGY

There is quite limited research within the POMS domain regarding the way LiDAR-based object and change detection could enhance operations in smart factories. Therefore, this study applies a qualitative case study approach, which is suitable for increasing the understanding of a phenomenon previously under investigated and thus to answer "how" questions [40]. The studied case includes the development of a solution concept for LiDAR-based object and change detection, its testing and collection of qualitative data on the research topic from the companies participating in the same project. VTT Technical Research Centre of Finland developed the technical solution. The solution is based on a LiDAR point-cloud comparison and helps identifying changes between the point clouds scanned at different times.

The solution can be used on a mobile platform, such as an AMR, which is moving around an industrial site anyway during its preliminary task (e.g., in intra-logistics). The aim is to develop a solution, which would enable mobile, real-time object and change detection in factories both indoors and outdoors. Parts of the solution were tested, and experiences gathered already in the course of this study, but development work is still ongoing based on the results so far. However, the solution concept is presented in this paper.

The solution was developed and tested in two phases. The first scanning round was done in real industrial environment outdoors on a factory yard. The changes that took place on the yard were related to the trash containers (present/absent), the factory doors (open/closed) and cars. The test results were gathered and used for further development. The version of the solution presented in this paper was finalized and tested again in office environment.

In addition to technical development work, qualitative data were gathered in discussions with company representatives. Nine companies attended the same publicly funded "Multi-purpose service robotics as operator business" R&D project in 2021-2022. The companies represent robotics, software and end-user companies. They attended several workshops during the research project, and among other research topics, they gave their views also into LiDAR object and change detection.

Tasks and results of this study are thus twofold: 1) Technical development work regarding the new mobile LiDAR-based object and change detection solution and its testing, and 2) identification of use cases in the production and operations management domain. Finally, conclusions were drawn combining onsite test results and discussions between the researchers and the company representatives on potential use cases and limitations of the solution.

IV. RESULTS

A. Solution concept for 3D LiDAR-based object and change detection

The large quantity of produced points by high resolution LiDARs makes the point-cloud processing a challenging task, especially if this is done in real-time. To achieve real-time change detection with this kind of high resolution LiDAR, we propose a solution that is based on an open-source C++ library called Open Visual Database System (OpenVDB) [41]. OpenVDB incorporates a hierarchical data structure and tools for the efficient storage and manipulation of sparse volumetric data maintained in 3D grids. This volumetric database is typically referred to as VDB. The library has been used in the visual effects industry for simulation and rendering of water, fire and other effects that rely on sparse volume data. Despite the wide use in numerous movie production applications over the last decade, the robotics community has paid little attention to the library. The proposed solution requires a reference point cloud to be converted to a NanoVDB level set grid as described in the steps of Figure 3.

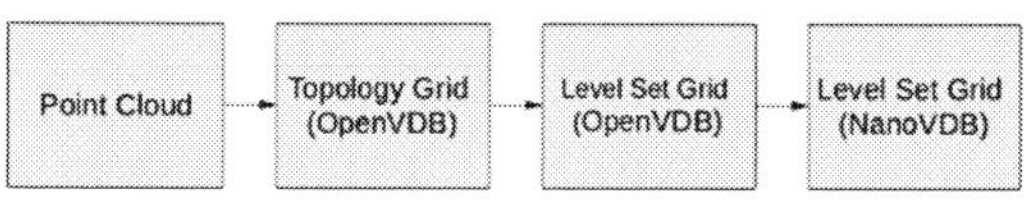

Figure 3. Steps to convert point cloud to NanoVDB level set.

NanoVDB [42] is a new addition to the OpenVDB library to leveragme the power of Graphics Processing Units (GPUs) in the processing of volumetric data, whereas OpenVDB was originally designed to be run Central Processing Unit (CPU) only. NanoVDB provides a simplified representation of the data structures being still completely compatible with the OpenVDB's tree structure. It offers functionality to convert back-and-forth between the NanoVDB and the OpenVDB data structures and to create and visualise the data. NanoVDB's compacted and linearised representation of the VDB tree structure is read-only. In other words, while values can be modified in a NanoVDB grid, its tree topology cannot. Despite this limitation, NanoVDB enables notably faster collision detection and raytracing compared to OpenVDB's CPU implementation [43]. The proposed approach for change detection follows the pipeline defined in Figure 4.

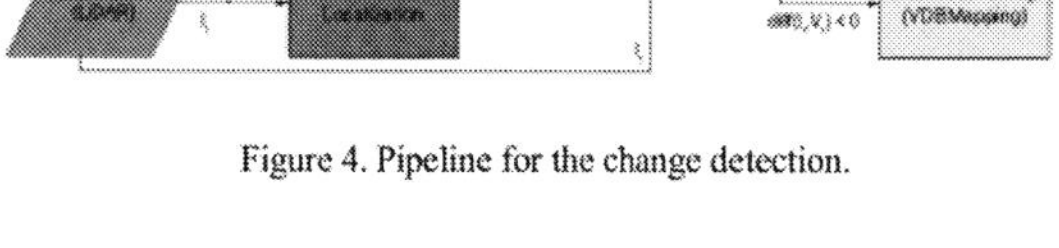

Figure 4. Pipeline for the change detection.

A NanoVDB level set grid is created from an existing 3D point cloud that represents the reference map of the environment. Because the same 3D point cloud is also used to localise the autonomously moving robot, the pose of the LiDAR scan can be used to render a matching virtual LiDAR scan from the NanoVDB level set grid. 3D localisation is done based on combining wheel or LiDAR odometry to a scan matching module that tries to minimise the cumulative drift of the odometry by registering the latest LiDAR scan or a submap created from multiple consecutive scans to the reference map [44].

The computationally expensive process of rendering virtual scans from an existing map of the environment is performed using NanoVDB on a GPU. For each new scan, the change detection is apprehended by calculating the difference between the LiDAR scan and the virtual LiDAR scan. The difference is defined according to range:

- range < 0: positive change (insert to OpenVDB grid as occluding voxel)
- range > 0: negative change (insert to OpenVDB grid as newly revealed voxel)
- range == 0: no change (optionally only update to NanoVDB grid as 'visible' voxels)

This way the positive and negative voxels are cumulated to the OpenVDB grid, done in the CPU as a NanoVDB grid cannot be modified. Afterwards, the changes are accumulated to OpenVDB grid via VDBMapping. In the following Figure 5 positive changes detected are presented:

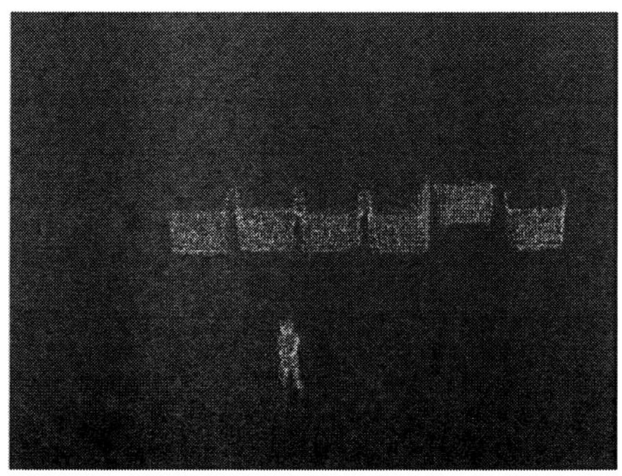

Figure 5. Positive changes detected at the industrial site.

The novelty of the presented method is in its approach to be real-time. The traditional method creates point clouds and only afterwards registers these to the same coordinate system and performs the change detection accordingly. Real-time approach enables more precise change detection on-site.

To the best of the authors' knowledge, NanoVDB is deployed in the field of robotics only to implement a GPU-accelerated mapping and simulation package called NanoMap [45]. This work extends the use of OpenVDB and NanoVDB to LiDAR-based change detection. Also, only in recent years, OpenVDB has been starting to appear in open source projects, e.g., to implement spatiotemporal occupancy grid map [46], probabilistic 3D mapping [47] and efficient Truncated Signed Distance Field (TSDF) integration of range sensor data [48]. The latter presents a 3D mapping library, called VDBFusion, which has a higher runtime, lower memory consumption and disc usage compared to older state-of-the-art 3D mapping libraries, like OctoMap [49] and Voxblox [50].

The presented work is evaluated on an embedded platform, NVIDIA Jetson AGX Orin, with data collected using two different robotic platforms, including SPOT robot (Figure 1) and ROVéo, ROVENSO's wheeled robot (Figure 6).

Figure 6. ROVENSO's ROVéo AMR.

B. *Identified use cases in production and operations management*

As results of this study, use cases for LiDAR-based object and change detection were identified. The emphasis is to complement data collected with fixed sensors in factories with LiDAR scans done continuously on a mobile platform. Real-time change detection is one central novelty value of the solution developed by VTT. When AMR detects relevant and defined changes in real-time, it can send an alarm for the respective organisation unit (e.g., security or production) with a location in which the change was detected so that the organisation can take the needed measures.

Another selection criterion for potential use cases was that purely LiDAR-based detection would be beneficial compared to camera or LiDAR-RGB camera-based detection and image recognition. Cameras and image detection is a more suitable method for detection of smaller details and items. Compared to visual light cameras, a relatively accurate 3D model of the environment can be created, and rather large items and changes can be detected. Another strength of LiDARs is in their use in poor lighting conditions. LiDARs are already commonly used in AGVs and AMRs, so no new sensor or camera investments would be needed, but the idea would be to better utilise data collected by those moving around in factories.

When identifying potential use cases for mobile LiDAR-based object and change detection, the following criteria and features of LiDAR-based detection were considered:

- Added value from AMR moving around the factory and factory site and detecting changes in real-time
- Achieving relatively accurate and up-to-date digital 3D reconstruction of the environment of the AMR with repeated LiDAR scans
- Visual detection of rather large physical items and changes
- LiDARs work also in poor or limited lighting conditions.

The next Table outlines identified use cases for LiDAR-based object and change detection in production and operations management:

TABLE I. INDUSTRIAL USE CASES FOR LIDAR-BASED OBJECT AND CHANGE DETECTION.

Industrial operation	**Use cases**
Internal logistics	- Pallets and other large items left in the wrong place - Blocked routes of AMRs and AGVs and sending information to the fleet management system or operators - Cars left in the wrong place (e.g., on AMR/AGV driving lanes) in the yard
Warehouse	- Pallets, trolleys or other large items left in the wrong place in the warehouse
Production	- Large items left in the wrong place on aisles or in production cells: links to lean, 5S and safety - Digital as-is 3D model as basis for machinery and production line modernisation
Security surveillance	- Blocked fire doors or large items left in the front of emergency exits that should be kept clean - Factory gate or open doors, e.g., at night when there or no people at work - Holes in factory area fence
Building maintenance	- As-is model of the factory as basis for factory renovation and modernisation and progress monitoring

V. CONCLUSIONS

RGB images and image recognition is often feasible for visual change detection [36]. However, in certain cases, an accurate digital 3D model of the environment created with LiDARs and detecting changes repeatedly in real-time accrue benefits for production and operations management. This study identified use cases for mobile, real-time LiDAR-based object and change detection. The new solution developed and presented enables efficient visual 3D data utilisation in operations management. The study shows practical implications of Industry 4.0 and 5.0 in terms of utilising autonomous systems and digital twins.

As the main results of the study, we identified potential use cases in production, internal logistics, security and maintenance operations for the developed solution. Identifying, e.g., obstacles on AGV and AMR routes and sending the information to the operators of fleet management systems helps AGVs and AMRs update their routes and continue their tasks smoothly. Thus, the solution may help in optimising traffic flows in factories. Detecting large items left in the wrong place and sending alarms for respective organisation units enhance intra-logistics operations, tidiness and safety. For security purposes, the solution identifies e.g. doors left open at nightime.

The study results contribute to the operations management literature [4]-[8] by presenting a new technical enabler for object and change detection in factories. The main novelty value of the solution is the aim of detecting changes in real-time on repetitive rounds of AMRs. Real-time approach enables more precise change detection on-site and provides many future development possibilities e.g. in terms of sending alarms of noted changes that might cause safety or other hazards. Thus, the results complement earlier studies on mobile change detection [33, 35]. Point cloud data collected with LiDARs will support more intelligent decision making in companies concerning, for example, production and intra-logistics [1][11][12].

As with any study, this one also has limitations. One limitation is that the technical solution is not ready yet, but is still under development. More testing and development will be needed in various industrial environments in order to ensure its reliability and accuracy. The accuracy of the change detection depends heavily on the accuracy of the 3D pose estimation of the LiDAR, which may be degraded due to measurement noise, motion distortion, and reflections from shiny surfaces. Moreover, major geometric changes in the environment (e.g., some walls removed) may also degrade the accuracy of the pose estimation. Another central limitation is that, in many cases, object and change detection is more feasible and cheaper to conduct with cameras. On the other hand, the use of LiDARs is already common in AGVs and AMRs, which reasons for wider utilisation of the data they collect. What remains important is to carefully evaluate which cases, e.g., RGB camera or RGB camera-LiDAR solution, are feasible and more reliable than a solution based solely on LiDAR. LiDARs' strengths remain in their ability to make a relatively accurate digital twin of the environment. Use cases that benefit from those have the foremost potential for LiDAR-based solutions.

Despite the limitations, this study inspires multiple interesting future R&D avenues. Within the production and operations management domain, autonomous systems, extensive data utilisation and so-called digital twins will provide much to study and develop in the future. For example, the fusion of multimodal data that AMRs collect can offer many possibilities for developing, e.g., manufacturing, intra-logistics and maintenance operations to be safer and more efficient. For example, one can integrate thermal camera and gas sensors onto a mobile robot platform, and data collected by those can be used in combination with LiDAR-generated maps for safety. More research will certainly arise from applying the new object and change detection method developed for various industries. Construction is one business field that would certainly benefit from real-time 3D modelling and change detection.

ACKNOWLEDGMENT

The MURO research project is funded by Business Finland, VTT and companies participating in the project.

REFERENCES

[1] B, Chen et al., "Smart factory of industry 4.0: Key technologies, application case, and challenges," IEEE Access, vol. 6, pp. 6505-6519, 2017.

[2] R. Morrar, H. Arman, and S. Mousa, "The fourth industrial revolution (Industry 4.0): A social innovation perspective," Technology innovation management review, vol. 7, no. 11, pp. 12-20, 2017.

[3] P. K. R. Maddikunta et al., "Industry 5.0: A survey on enabling technologies and potential applications," Journal of Industrial Information Integration, vol. 26, pp. 1-19, 2022.

[4] Z. M Bi and L. Wang, "Advances in 3D data acquisition and processing for industrial applications," Robotics and Computer-Integrated Manufacturing, vol. 26, no. 5, pp. 403-413, 2010.

[5] G. Fragapane, R. De Koster, F. Sgarbossa, and J. O. Strandhagen, "Planning and control of autonomous mobile robots for intralogistics: Literature review and research agenda," European Journal of Operational Research, vol. 294, no. 2, pp. 405-426, 2021.

[6] V. De Silva, J. Roche, and A. Kondoz, "Robust fusion of LiDAR and wide-angle camera data for autonomous mobile robots," Sensors, vol. 18, no. 8, pp. 2730, 2018.

[7] T. Yang et al., "3D ToF LiDAR in mobile robotics: a review," arXiv preprint arXiv:2202.11025, 2022.

[8] D. Zhang, J. Cao, G. Dobie, and C. MacLeod, "A framework of using customized LIDAR to localize robot for nuclear reactor inspections," IEEE Sensors Journal, vol. 22, no. 6, pp. 5352-5359, 2021.

[9] T. M. Choi, S. Kumar, X. Yue, and H. L. Chan, "Disruptive technologies and operations management in the Industry 4.0 era and beyond," Production and Operations Management, vol. 31, no. 1, pp. 9-31, 2022.

[10] H. Lasi, P. Fettke, H. G. Kemper, T. Feld, and M. Hoffmann, "Industry 4.0. Business & information systems engineering," vol. 6, no. 4, pp. 239-242, 2014.

[11] D. Bertsimas, N. Kallus, and A. Hussain (2016), "Inventory management in the era of big data," Production and Operations Management, vol. 25, no. 12, pp. 2006-2009, 2014.

[12] T. M. Choi, S. W. Wallace, and Y. Wang, "Big data analytics in operations management," Prod. Oper. Manag. vol. 27, no. 10, pp. 1868–1883, 2018.

[13] K. Shafique, B. A. Khawaja, F. Sabir, S. Qazi, and M. Mustaqim, "Internet of things (IoT) for next-generation smart systems: A review of current challenges, future trends and prospects for emerging 5G-IoT scenarios," Ieee Access, vol. 8, pp. 23022-23040, 2020.

[14] T. L. Olsen and B. Tomlin, "Industry 4.0: Opportunities and challenges for operations management," Manufacturing & Service Operations Management, vol. 22, no. 1, pp. 113-122, 2020.

[15] E. Guerra, R. Munguía, and A. Grau, "UAV visual and laser sensors fusion for detection and positioning in industrial applications," Sensors, vol. 18, no.7, pp. 2071, 2018.

[16] P. Wei, L. Cagle, T. Reza, J. Ball, and J. Gafford, "LiDAR and camera detection fusion in a real-time industrial multi-sensor collision avoidance system," Electronics, vol. 7, no. 6, pp. 84, 2018.

[17] C. Debeunne and D. Vivet, "A review of visual-LiDAR fusion based simultaneous localization and mapping," Sensors, vol. 20, no. 7, pp. 2068, 2020.

[18] W. Lu, Y. Zhou, G. Wan, S. Hou, and S. Song "L3-net: Towards learning based lidar localization for autonomous driving," Proceedings of the IEEE/CVF Conference on Computer Vision and Pattern Recognition, pp. 6389-6398, 2019.

[19] D. Van Nam and K. Gon-Woo, "Solid-state LiDAR based-SLAM: A concise review and application," 2021 IEEE International Conference on Big Data and Smart Computing (BigComp), pp. 302-305, 2021.

[20] S. Gargoum and K. El-Basyouny "Automated extraction of road features using LiDAR data: A review of LiDAR applications in transportation," In 2017 4th International Conference on Transportation Information and Safety (ICTIS), pp. 563-574. IEEE, August 2017.

[21] S. A. Gargoum and K. El Basyouny, "A literature synthesis of LiDAR applications in transportation: Feature extraction and geometric assessments of highways," GIScience & Remote Sensing, vol. 56, no.6, pp. 864-893, 2019.

[22] H. Guan, J. Li, S. Cao, and Y. Yu, "Use of mobile LiDAR in road information inventory: A review. International Journal of Image and Data Fusion", vol. 7, no. 3, pp. 219-242, 2016.

[23] T. Neumann, A. Ferrein, S. Kallweit, and I. Scholl, "Towards a mobile mapping robot for underground mines," Proceedings of the 2014 PRASA, RobMech and AfLaT International Joint Symposium, Cape Town, South Africa, pp. 27-28, 2014.

[24] R. Zlot and M. Bosse, "Efficient large-scale 3D mobile mapping and surface reconstruction of an underground mine," Field and service robotics, pp. 479-493, Springer, Berlin, Heidelberg, 2014.

[25] M. Awrangjeb, "Effective generation and update of a building map database through automatic building change detection from LiDAR point cloud data," Remote Sensing, vol. 7, no. 10, pp. 14119-14150, 2015.

[26] J. L. Blanco-Claraco, F. A. Moreno-Duenas, and J. González-Jiménez, "The Málaga urban dataset: High-rate stereo and LiDAR in a realistic urban scenario," The International Journal of Robotics Research, vol. 33, no. 2, pp. 207-214, 2014.

[27] A. Börcs, B. Nagy, and C. Benedek, "Instant object detection in lidar point clouds," IEEE Geoscience and Remote Sensing Letters, vol. 14, no. 7, pp. 992-996, 2017.

[28] X. Meng, N. Currit, L. Wang, and X. Yang, "Detect residential buildings from lidar and aerial photographs through object-oriented land-use classification," Photogrammetric Engineering & Remote Sensing, vol. 78, no.1, pp. 35-44, 2012.

[29] J. Schreyer, J. Tigges, T. Lakes, and G. Churkina, "Using airborne LiDAR and QuickBird data for modelling urban tree carbon storage and its distribution—A case study of Berlin," Remote Sensing, vol. 6, no. 11, pp. 10636-10655, 2014.

[30] U. Weiss and P. Biber, "Plant detection and mapping for agricultural robots using a 3D LIDAR sensor," Robotics and autonomous systems, vol. 59, no. 5, pp. 265-273, 2011.

[31] A. S. Chase, D. Z. Chase, and A. F Chase, "LiDAR for archaeological research and the study of historical landscapes," Sensing the Past, pp. 89-100. Springer, Cham, 2017.

[32] J. P. Underwood, D. Gillsj¨o, T. Bailey, and V. Vlaskine, "Explicit 3d change detection using ray-tracing in spherical coordinates," 2013 IEEE international conference on robotics and automation, pp. 4735–4741. IEEE, 2013.

[33] W. Xiao, B. Vallet, K. Schindler, and N. Paparoditis, "Street-side vehicle detection, classification and change detection using mobile laser scanning data," ISPRS Journal of Photogrammetry and Remote Sensing, vol. 114, pp. 166-178, 2016.

[34] Y. Wu, Y. Wang, S. Zhang, and H. Ogai, "Deep 3D object detection networks using LiDAR data: A review," IEEE Sensors Journal, vol. 21, no. 2, pp. 1152-1171, 2020.

[35] I. Jinno, Y. Sasaki, and H. Mizoguchi, "3d map update in human environment using change detection from lidar equipped mobile robot," 2019 IEEE/SICE International Symposium on System Integration (SII) (pp. 330-335). IEEE.

[36] K. Simonyan and A. Zisserman, "Very deep convolutional networks for large-scale image recognition," arXiv preprint arXiv:1409.1556, 2014.

[37] A. H. Lang, S. Vora, H. Caesar, L. Zhou, J. Yang, and O. Beijbom, "PointPillars: Fast encoders for object detection from point clouds," In Proceedings of the IEEE Conference on Computer Vision and Pattern Recognition, Long Beach, CA, USA, pp. 12697–12705, June 2019.

[38] Y. Zhou et al., "End-to-end multi-view fusion for 3d object detection in lidar point clouds," Conference on Robot Learning, pp. 923-932, 2020.

[39] H. Kuang, B. Wang, J. An, M. Zhang, and Z. Zhang, "Voxel-FPN: Multi-scale voxel feature aggregation for 3D object detection from LIDAR point clouds," Sensors, vol. 20, no. 3, pp. 704, 2020.

[40] R. K. Yin. Case study research—Design and methods. Thousand Oaks: Sage Publications, 2003.

[41] K. Museth et al. "Openvdb: an open-source data structure and toolkit for high-resolution volumes," in Acm siggraph 2013 courses, pp. 1–1, 2013.

[42] K. Museth, "Nanovdb: A gpu-friendly and portable vdb data structure for real-time rendering and simulation," ACM SIGGRAPH 2021 Talks, pp. 1-2, 2021.

[43] W. Braithwaite and K. Muset, "NVIDIA Technical Blog: Accelerating OpenVDB on GPUs with NanoVDB", https://developer.nvidia.com/blog/accelerating-openvdb-on-gpus-with-nanovdb/. Accessed: 2022-12-02.

[44] D. Rozenberszki and A. L. Majdik, "LOL: Lidar-only Odometry and Localization in 3D point cloud maps", IEEE International Conference on Robotics and Automation (ICRA), pp. 4379-4385, 2020.

[45] V. Walker, F. Vanegas, and F. Gonzalez, "NanoMap: A gpu-accelerated openvdb-based mapping and simulation hpackage for robotic agents," Remote Sensing, voil. 14, no. 21, pp. 5463, 2022.

[46] S. Macenski, D. Tsai, and M. Feinberg, "Spatiotemporal voxel layer: A view on robot perception for the dynamic world," International Journal of Advanced Robotic Systems, vol. 17, no. 2, pp. 1-14, 2020.

[47] M. Grosse Besselmann, L. Puck, L. Steffen, A. Roennau, and R. Dillmann, "Vdb-mapping: A high resolution and real-time capable 3d mapping framework for versatile mobile robots," 2021 IEEE 17th International Conference on Automation Science and Engineering (CASE), pp. 448–454. IEEE, 2021.

[48] V. Ignacio, T. Guadagnino, J. Behley, and C. Stachniss. Vdbfusion, "Flexible and efficient tsdf integration of range sensor data," Sensors, vol. 22, no. 3, pp. 1-24, 2022.

[49] A. Hornung, K. M. Wurm, M. Bennewitz, C. Stachniss, and W. Burgard, "Octomap: An efficient probabilistic 3d mapping framework based on octrees," Autonomous robots, vol. 3, no. 3, pp. 189-206, 2013.

[50] H. Oleynikova, Z. Taylor, M. Fehr, R. Siegwart, and J. Nieto, "Voxblox: Incremental 3d euclidean signed distance fields for on-board mav planning," IEEE/RSJ International Conference on Intelligent Robots and Systems (IROS), pp. 1366-1373. IEEE, 2017.

Simulated Ant-agent Aspects for Defining an Ant-bots Ontology

Colin Chibaya
Sol Plaatje University
Kimberley, South Africa
Email: colin.chibaya@spu.ac.za

Ntsuxeko Shirindi
Sol Plaatje University
Kimberley, South Africa
Email: 202112339@spu.ac.za

Rifilwe Modiba
Sol Plaatje University
Kimberley, South Africa
Email: Rifilwe.modiba@spu.ac.za

***Abstract*—Swarm intelligence systems, wherein robotic devices encoded with collections of discrete abilities executed at individual levels to cause swarm level emergent behaviour are appealing to fields, such as nanotechnology. Such swarm intelligence systems are typically used to solve complex real-life problems at, often, minimal costs. For example, ant colony systems have been proposed for deriving solutions to tough problems by emulating the behaviours of natural ants. Solutions to complex optimisation problems such as the bridge crossing problem, vehicle routing problems, shortest path formation problem, and travelling salesman problem have been presented. This study takes inspiration from the various simulated ant colony systems, investigating the low-level actions and abilities of simulated ant-like robotic devices towards prescribing an ant-bots swarm intelligence ontology. In this context, an ant-bot is assumed to be a tiny naive autonomous robotic device built on the characteristics of simulated ants. On its own, an ant-bot would not achieve anything practical. However, as a swarm, ant-bots can create compelling emergent behaviour. We investigate the discrete aspects of simulated ant agents that cause emergent behaviour and explicitly cogitate them in the design of an ant-bots swarm intelligence ontology. Experimental tests connoted three such aspects as the building blocks of the desired swarm intelligence ontology. First, the swarm space captures metadata about the configuration of the simulated environments, targets, and any global swarm rules. On the other hand, ant-bot context emphasizes the individual abilities and activities of ant-bots. Last, the swarm interaction aspect apprehends the embraced communication mechanism, whether direct or indirect, local, or global, nature inspired, mathematical, biological, or otherwise. Commendably, the swarm intelligence ontology thereof is a mere formal ant-bot knowledge representation model.**

Keywords:* *ant-bot; swarm intelligence; ant-bot ontology.

I. INTRODUCTION

Swarm intelligence focuses on the design of intelligent multi-agent systems based on the collective natural behaviour of social colonies, such as ants, termites, birds, spiders, and bees [1]. It is a comparatively recent problem-solving method that draws inspiration from nature [2]. However, the methods governing the behaviour of natural colonies remains unknown. Although cooperative colony behaviour emerges from relatively straightforward relationships between the colony members, what exactly does each member do to cause colony level behaviour?

Ants are fascinating. Related ant systems have received much attention because of their practical application to combinatorial optimisation problems [4] such as shortest path formation [5]. However, what does each simulated ant agent do for swarm convergence? How do we formalize the representation of the knowledge insinuated in ant systems towards a more visible practical use in real life problem solving?

An ontology is a philosophical branch that investigates the concepts of existence, being, becoming, and reality [6]. A swarm intelligence ontology, therefore, refers to a collection of the swarm knowledge related to swarm members behaviour, swarm member abilities, the environment in which the swarm is deployed, as well as all the other meta parameters of the swarm. This study seeks to understand the design of an ant systems inspired swarm intelligence ontology.

A. *Problem statement*

Creating an ant-bots ontology connotes coordination of homogeneous swarms. Pushing this agenda further to the coordination of heterogeneous swarms is an ambitious project which involves understanding various discrete swarm intelligence ontologies. For example, we would require independent ants, termites, bees, social spiders, fish, or birds ontologies before we build a generic swarm intelligence ontology that may tackle heterogeneity.

Simulated ant systems are fascinating. What are the building blocks of an ant-bots ontology that may contribute to the development of heterogeneity in the swarm intelligence body of knowledge?

Little has been said about ant-bots abilities to create emergent behaviour. Individual actions of ant-bots, communication, interaction strategies, decision-making, and the information they generate are blurred ingredients of swarm knowledge. Representation of this knowledge has not, yet, been formalized, which is the theme of this study. The article seeks to pinpoint and characterize the key aspects of simulated ant systems that define an ant-bots ontology. Achieving this involves conceptualization of the environment in which ant-bots operate, the design of the ant-bots, and an understanding of the processes through which ant-bots interact, communicate, share, or create knowledge. In the end, we seek to demonstrate an informed understanding of the prospective vocabulary of ant-bots towards improved application and visibility of ant systems. To the best of our knowledge, formalized representation of ant systems in the form of an ontology is a creative intervention in the field.

B. Overview

The article is structured as follows: Section II presents literature which identifies the predominant ant system aspects that may inspire the design of an ant-bots ontology. Section III goes on to characterize the identified aspects, taking us closer to pinpointing the component units of the envisioned ant-bots ontology. In Section IV, the actual ant-bots ontology is proposed before we conclude the study in Section V, highlighting the contributions we make, as well as pointing the direction for future work.

II. RELATED WORK

Research intervention to represent knowledge substantively and methodologically is visible [8]. Although we note attempts in the literature to create swarm intelligence ontologies inspired by the functionalities of ant colony systems, bee colony optimisation models, particle swarm optimisation systems, and even heuristic particle swarm ant colony optimization models, such specificity and explicitness in the representation of ant-bots knowledge is still blurred. This study seeks to investigate specific aspects of simulated ant systems to then suggest an explicit ant-bots ontology.

Closest in the literature are works that investigated the meaning or purpose of pheromones in directing ant-like agents moving between two points [2]. These works established pheromones as indirect guides towards agents' targets. Pheromone mark the paths ant agents probabilistically follow. Directions are selected stochastically based on the levels of pheromone around a decision-making ant agent. We refer to direction selection by ant-bots as orientation. This understanding of the meaning of pheromone as guides to ant agents has been modified and optimized many times [9]. Although all the hybrids yielded maintain the same concept of pheromone perception for orientation, heuristic information is required to bring about optimal solutions [10][23]. For example, defining swarm memory abstractly as held on the environment is a heuristic feature to merely reducing the cost of managing ant-bots.

Most ant systems insinuate ant agents that also possess some internal state in which to keep the swarm goal [19]. Each ant agent is always aware of its target, implying knowledge of which levels of pheromone are attractive or repulsive at the time [19]. Therefore, flipping between different internal states is a reward that comes with an ant agent finding the target or successfully returning to the nest [19][21]. During the search for the target or nest, it is a standard that ant agents drop and update specific levels of pheromone depending on their internal state [10][22]. Pheromone updates are also heuristically administered through dissipation processes [19] to optimize swarm convergence quality and speed. Summarily, most ant systems achieve mission planning and execution through (a) pheromone management policies (detection of the levels of pheromone around, dropping new levels of pheromone at current location, updating the quantities of pheromone held at current location, and pheromone dissipation), (b) internal state transitions (heuristically managing context awareness, and ant agents flipping between internal states when it becomes necessary), as well as (c) local search procedures (orientation and movements).

A survey of the theoretical meaning of ant colony optimisation [11] has also been presented. Emphasis has been on understanding the theoretical basis of swarm convergence on optimal solutions given that stochastic methods drive the processes. However, trust level computation demonstrated in [12] notably insinuated the value of similar swarm aspects for recommendation towards an ant-bots ontology [13]. The primary goal of this study is to explicitly elucidate the key aspects of ant systems that may inspire the design of ant-bots ontology for more visible application of related swarm intelligence systems in real life.

III. METHODS

This study is still in the infancy towards the creation of heterogeneous ontologies. It focuses on understanding a particular homogeneous ant-bot ontology that will be integrated with other homogeneous ontologies towards addressing heterogeneity in swarm intelligence models. Precisely, we conduct (a) a requirements elicitation exercise (seeking for what matters in the design of an ant-bots ontology), (b) requirements specification (looking at how each elicited aspect fits into the problem) and (c) administer the ontology modelling and proposing a methodology for integrating these aspects.

Design science research is adopted when the main computational artifacts of the study are defined [14]. In proposing the ant-bots ontology, emphasis is invested on achieving scalability, reproducibility, and adaptability. A positivist school of thoughts drives the study towards understanding the veracity of the work [15] through deductive means [16][17] until an ant-bots ontology ensues. Hopefully, the results we yield should be transferable from views to theory [18]. The next sub-sections give detailed analyses of those aspects prevalently insinuated when ant systems are studied.

A. Ant-bot architecture

An ant-bot is designed with basic memory in which to hold four key pieces of information pertaining to its position, internal state, neighbourhood, and the available instruction set as shown in Figure 1. Awareness of the current position allows an ant-bot to retrieve the levels of pheromone held on that position. It allows the ant-bot to be able to update specific levels of pheromone at its location in specific quantities. Positional awareness is an individual ant-bot property.

The internal state keeps the ant-bot's purpose in the swarm. At any point, an ant-bot is either searching for the target or travelling back to the nest. In each mode, an ant-bot places a different type of pheromone on its current position, thus updating the swarm's global information. Often, an ant-bot places pheromones attractive to other ant-bots in the opposite internal state mode. For example, an ant-bot searching for the target places pheromones that are attractive to ant-bots that are travelling back to the nest. Those ant-bots travelling to the nest places pheromones that are attractive to

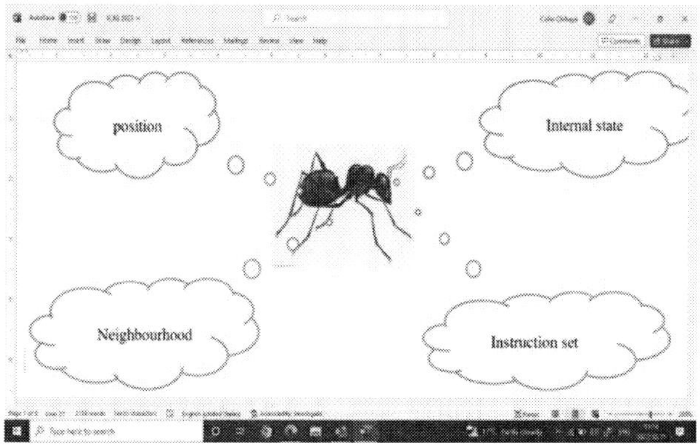

Figure 1. Ant-bot design

ant-bots searching for the target. That way, trodden paths emerge at swarm levels.

Also, every ant-bot is designed with the ability to perceive its neighbourhood. The neighbourhood comprises candidate locations an ant-bot may move to. Each location in the neighbourhood is assigned some weight based on its attractiveness or repulsiveness. Such attractiveness or repulsiveness of nearby locations is based on the amounts of specific levels of pheromone they hold. An ant-bot stochastically decides on where to go based on the attractiveness or repulsiveness of the locations around it.

Last, ant-bots follow deterministic instructions to achieve their goals. They are designed with the ability to follow these instructions at individual level towards achieving swarm level emergent behaviour. A collection of these instructions and their parameters is described further in the next section on ant-bots actions. This work does not dwell on the engineering side of the design of ant-bots.

B. Ant-bots actions

It is apparent that ant-bots drop specific levels of pheromone as they navigate the environment. The action of dropping pheromone updates the quantities of this specific level of pheromone held on the ant-bot's current location. The quantity of pheromone held on the environment creates a shared memory for the swarm. Holding these quantities on the environment has the advantage of freeing ant-bots from the need to have large memory capacity. It also separates the ant-bot's life from the swarm solution. When an ant-bot drops and updates specific levels of pheromone at its current location, that action also updates the swarm level shared memory. Listing 1 presents the concept of dropping pheromone in computational terms.

Listing 1: dropping levels of pheromone

```
Drop (int x, int y, int Qty)
{
  update(level,Qty + read (level, x, y))

}
```

Precisely, an ant-bot reads the quantity of the levels of pheromone, at current location, that are repulsive at the time, and update the same levels by a prescribed quantity.

The next step for an ant-bot would be to relocate, after dropping specific levels of pheromone at the current position. This requires an ant-bot to, first, orientate before following some direction. Orientation, in computation terms, refers to an ant-bot detecting the attractiveness or repulsiveness of neighbouring locations before choosing a direction. This is achieved by weighting neighbouring locations based of the levels of attractive and repulsive pheromone they hold. Locations that have more attractive than repulsive levels are favoured while those locations with more repulsive than attractive levels are penalized. Listing 2 presents the concept of orientation algorithmically.

Listing 2: ant-bot orientation

```
Orientate (int x, int y)
{
  for each nearbyLocation i
  {
  wi←qtyAtt(x±[0,1];y±[0,1])-qtyRep(x±[0,1];y±[0,1])
  }
    set a scaled roulette wheel for wi
      direction ← randPick (i,wi)
}
```

The equation in the loop in listing 2 shows how the weight of each location around an ant-bot is calculated. Once these weights are known, a stochastic roulette wheel is established where more attractive locations are allocated wider spans than repulsive locations. Random selection of a location in such a setup favour selection of attractive rather than repulsive locations. Great in this approach is that even very repulsive locations can still be stochastically picked to bring about randomness in the movement. However, it would be rare that a repulsive location gets picked.

Ant-bot movement follows successful orientation. Movement is about relocation in the orientation direction. The aspect of movement is interpreted in listing 3.

Listing 3: ant-bot movement

```
Move (int x, int y, direction i)
{
   x ← x + direction (ix)
   y ← y + direction (iy)
}
```

In this case, an ant-bot would move from its x coordinate towards the x direction of the direction of orientation. It would move from its y coordinate towards the y direction of the direction of orientation.

Eventually and at some point, a moving ant-bot will hit its target. This achievement triggers the flip state action. An ant-bot that was searching for a food target would change its role in the swarm to start looking for the nest. It would change its perception of which pheromone is attractive and repulsive. Also, it would flip the levels of pheromone it drops on visited locations, assuming opposite phenomena thereafter. Listing 4 describes flipping between different internal states.

```
Listing 4: ant-bot flip state

state Flip (int x, int y)
{
    if (x ; y) has Target
     return homing
    if (x ; y) has Nest
     return searching
}
```

Precisely, this aspect conditionally returns a particular internal state depending on the location of the ant-bot at the time. An ant-bot that finds itself at the target because it was searching for a target should change to homing, where it starts the journey back to the nest. An ant-bot that finds itself at the nest because it has been homing should flip to the searching mode and commence the search trips all over. This function will only have effects on these two targets. Otherwise, a searching ant – bot that has not found the target would continue searching. An ant-bot travelling the nest, that has not reached the nest, will continue homing until it finds the nest. A collection of all ant-bot actions from the ant-bots instruction set was shown in Figure 1 earlier on.

C. Heuristic aspects

The ant-bot systems utilize two key heuristic elements. These swarms of ant-bots operate in deterministic environments that include specific locations, pheromone levels, and the context in which the ant-bots exist or navigate as they solve problems. The environment serves as a shared memory for the swarm. Figure 2 shows an example of this environment, depicted as a grid of locations where the ant-bots can move and leave pheromone behind. The parameters of this environment are set during the simulation process.

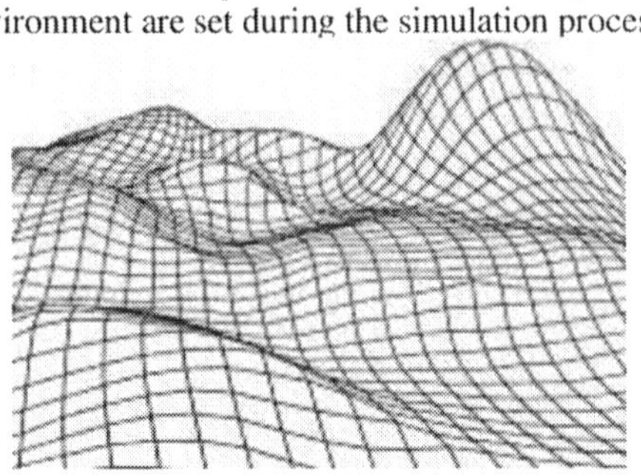

Figure 2. Ant-bots environments

Interesting is that the pheromone levels dropped on different locations of the environment may virtually dissipate through evaporation or diffusion. Pheromone dissipation is an elitist approach for smoothen the pheromone paths formed. It is also a mechanism with which old solutions may be forgotten in favour of new outcomes. Although these aspects are not directly associated with the life of an ant-bot, they contribute to ant-bot behaviours, hence required in the design of an ant-bots ontology.

IV. ANT-BOT ONTOLOGY

Figure 3 visualizes the integration of ant-bots architecture, ant-bots actions, and the related heuristic aspects into an ant-bot ontology. The proposed ontology primarily shows the locations of different pieces of ant-bot knowledge. The centre or core of the ontology holds the

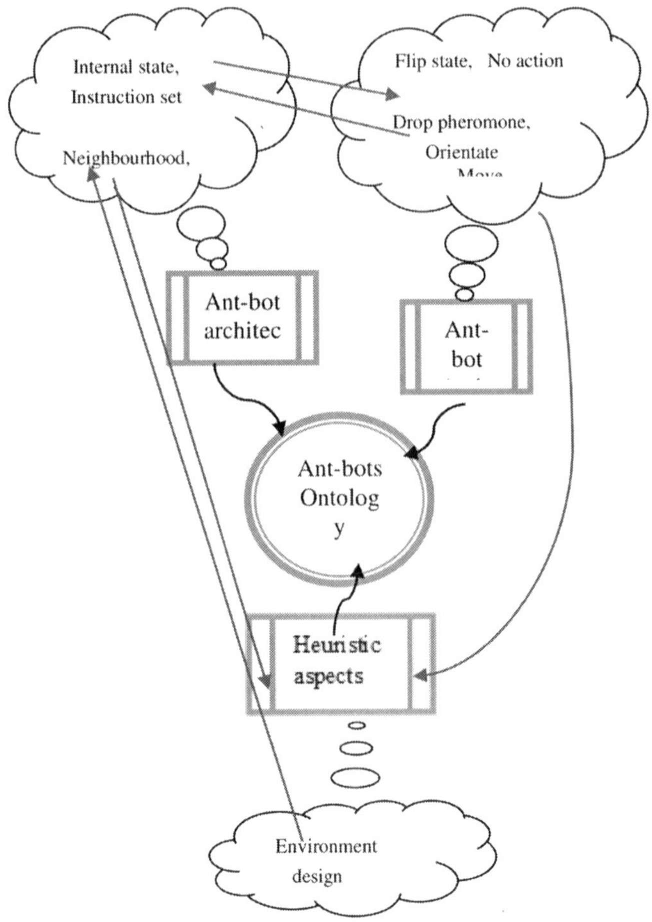

Figure 3. Ant-bots ontology

widespread representation of swarm level knowledge which synchronizes knowledge from the supporting sub-domains. The heuristic aspects have to do with environmental designs and how the pheromone levels deposited on the environment are maintained and smoothened beyond ant-bot abilities. Also, the core is aided by the ant-bot architecture which captures positional knowledge, internal states details about each ant-bot recalling its goal in the swarm, its neighbourhood, and how each ant-bot uses the instructions held in the ant-bots actions knowledge domain. The instructions include actions such as drop pheromone, move, orientate, and flip state.

It is pertinent to note that the survival of an ant-bots swarm depends on the strength of the shared memory defined by the levels of pheromone held on the environment. Low levels of pheromone on the environment connote lack of swarm level knowledge of the location of the target, hence random movements. On the other hand, excess levels of pheromone would saturate the environment and deplete the formed paths. A balance is struck through elitist heuristic means, including pheromone dissipation.

In this study, we do not concentrate on detailing implementational concerns. Instead, we are concerned with the logic for emulating ant behaviour. We want to focus on figuring out what each ant-bot does at an individual level to achieve swarm level emergent behaviour. We are concerned with the understanding of homogeneous swarms of ant-bots where each is simple and autonomous. In this case, the ontology connotes only stigmergic communication indirectly mediated via the environment [19][20]. None of the ant-bots can pass direct messages to others. However, it is possible that an ant-bot may choose not to do anything when it becomes necessary, hence inclusion of a No action aspect in the ant-bot instruction set.

V. CONCLUSION

This article investigated those aspects of ant systems that cause emergent behaviour and interpreted each in computational perspectives. It went on to suggest a way of putting those aspects together into a knowledge representation framework which we referred to as an ant-bots ontology. The ant-bots ontology is envisioned to capture all the key aspects for coordinating swarms of homogeneous ant-like robotic devices. Unfolding the elements of the ant-bots ontology is essential to providing a detailed modelling scenario that can be applied to other swarm formations. Precisely, the clarity sought in the design of the ant-bots ontology can propel application-specific modelling of solutions to practical problems. The ant-bots ontology presented in this article comprises three knowledge domains which are interrelated to the core domain. These three aspects, together with their relational inferences form the ant-bots ontology.

A. *Contributions*

Three contributions emanate from this study as follows:

- The article suggested a formal knowledge representation approach for defining ant inspired swarm intelligence systems. This literature extends content in the field.
- Proposals aimed at formalizing knowledge representation in swarm intelligence models are upcoming. This work is one of many studies aimed at understanding the key knowledge domains of swarm intelligence systems, focusing on ant systems. Although this is a discrete case, it guides us towards generic views.
- Although the focus was on understanding an ontology for a homogeneous swarm of ant-bots, the work creates a baseline upon which heterogeneity may be tackled.

B. *Future work*

Four ambitious directions for future work are envisioned from this study as follows:

- Corroboration of ant-bot knowledge representation through practical experimentation is upcoming.
- An ant-bot ontology could be enriched through incorporation of applicable aspects to cover a wider scope of use cases. It must be tested for completeness, optimality, applicability, and expandability.
- Integration of the ant-bots ontology with other swarm intelligence ontologies may, eventually, bring about practical heterogeneous swarms.
- It is worth pursuing the extensibility of the ant-bots ontology to deal with fuzzy situations, uncertainty, incompleteness, inaccuracies, vagueness, or impreciseness.

ACKNOWLEDGMENT

We acknowledge both the moral and technical support given by the Sol Plaatje University, department of Computer Science, Data Science, and Information Technology. This research was funded by the ABSA research grant, as well as the CAIR project (Centre for Artificial Intelligence Research) grant, with the grant agreement number: CSIR/BEI/HNP/CAIR/2020/10, supported by the Government of the Republic of South Africa, through its Department of Science and Innovation (DSI).

REFERENCES

[1] V. Selvi and R. Umarani. "Comparative analysis of ant colony and particle swarm optimization techniques". In: International Journal of Computer Applica- tions 5.4 (2010).

[2] M. Dorigo, M. Birattari, and T. Stutzle. "Ant colony optimiza- tion". In: IEEE computational intelligence magazine 1.4 (2006).

[3] S. Mittal and L. Rainey. "Harnessing emergence: The control and design of emergent behavior in system of systems engineering". In: Proceed- ings of the conference on summer computer simulation. 2015.

[4] M. Dorigo and C. Blum. "Ant colony optimization theory: A sur- vey". In: Theoretical computer science 344.2-3 (2005).

[5] A. Kaveh and S. Talatahari. "An improved ant colony optimization for con- strained engineering design problems". In: Engineering Computations (2010).

[6] K. Moon and D. Blackman. "A guide to understanding social science research for natural scientists". In: Conservation biology 28.5 (2014).

[7] J. Wang and G. Beni. "Cellular robotic system with stationary robots and its application to manufacturing lattices". In: Proceedings. IEEE Interna- tional Symposium on Intelligent Control 1989. IEEE. 1989.

[8] A. Booth. "Searching for qualitative research for inclusion in system- atic reviews: a structured methodological review". In: Systematic reviews 5.1 (2016).

[9] J. Wang, X. L. Fan, and H. Ding. "An improved ant colony optimization approach for optimization of process planning". In: The Scientific World Journal 2014.

[10] V. Maniezzo, L M Gambardella, and F. D Luigi. New Optimization Techniques in Engineering, ch. Ant Colony Optimization. 2004.

[11] M. Dorigo and C. Blum. "Ant colony optimization theory: A survey". In: Theoretical computer science 344.2-3 (2005).

[12] K. Moon and D. Blackman. "A guide to understanding social science research for natural scientists". In: Conservation biology 28.5 (2014).

[13] O. Deepa and A. Senthilkumar. "Swarm intelligence from natural to artificial systems: Ant colony optimization". In: Networks (Graph-Hoc) 8.1 (2016).

[14] V. R. Reddy and A. R. Reddy. "Lifetime Improvement of WSN by Trust Level based Ant Colony Optimization". In: International Journal of Computer Science and Information Technologies 5.5 (2014).

[15] G. M. Sinatra and D. Lombardi. "Evaluating sources of scientific evidence and claims in the post-truth era may require reappraising plausibility judgments". In: Educational Psychologist 55.3 (2020).

[16] A. M. Novikov and D. A. Novikov. Research methodology: From philosophy of science to research design. Vol. 2. CRC Press, 2013.

[17] G. Malhotra. "Strategies in research". In: International Journal for Advance Research and Development 2.5 (2017).

[18] A. D. Kramer, J. E. Guillory, and J. T. Hancock. "Experimental evidence of massive-scale emotional contagion through social networks". In: Proceedings of the National Academy of Sciences 111.24 (2014).

[19] M. B. Varsha, M. Kumar, and N. Kumar. "Hybrid TABU-GA search for energy efficient routing In WSN". In: International Journal of Recent Tech- nology and Engineering (IJRTE) 8.4 (2019).

[20] A. J. Hepworth, D. P. Baxter and H. A. Abbass. "Onto4MAT: A Swarm Shepherding Ontology for Generalized Multiagent Teaming". In IEEE Access, vol. 10, pp. 59843-59861, doi: 10.1109/ACCESS.2022.3180032. (2022).

[21] A. Kornrumpf and U. Baumöl, "A Design Science Approach to Collective Intelligence Systems," 2014 47th Hawaii International Conference on System Sciences, Waikoloa, HI, USA, pp. 361-370, doi: 10.1109/HICSS.2014.53. (2014).

[22] S. Kazadi, A. Wen and M. Volodarsky, "Reliable Swarm Design," 2009 17th Mediterranean Conference on Control and Automation, Thessaloniki, Greece, pp. 1301-1306, doi: 10.1109/MED.2009.5164726. (2009).,

[23] S. Kazadi and J. Lee. "Swarm Economics". In: Ao, SI., Rieger, B., Chen, SS. (eds) Advances in Computational Algorithms and Data Analysis. Lecture Notes in Electrical Engineering, vol 14. Springer, Dordrecht. (2009).

Toward Autonomous Cardiac Catheterization Through a Parametric Finite Element Simulation With Experimental Validation

Majid Roshanfar
Department of Mechanical Engineering
Concordia University
Montreal, Canada
e-mail: m_roshan@encs.concordia.ca

Pedram Fekri
Department of Mechanical Engineering
Concordia University
Montreal, Canada
e-mail: p_fekri@encs.concordia.ca

Javad Dargahi
Department of Mechanical Engineering
Concordia University
Montreal, Canada
e-mail: dargahi@encs.concordia.ca

***Abstract*—Catheters are thin tubes or wires made of medical-grade materials that are inserted through small incisions into the human body. In order to have a safe and effective robot-assisted radio frequency ablation, a real-time force estimator is required to measure the applied forces at the tip of the catheter. Finite element analysis can provide the real-time contact force of the steerable catheter. To do so, a nonlinear planar finite element model of the steerable catheter was first developed using parametric material properties in ANSYS software. After that, a series of finite element simulations based on each mechanical property was performed, and the deformed shape of the catheter was recorded. Next, the performance was validated by comparing the outputs of the simulation with experimental results from setup. In fact, the validation force was between the range 0 and 0.45 N that determined the material properties of the catheter. The results of the proposed finite element model were in fair agreement with reference values from the experiment. The proposed method met the requirements for autonomous cardiac ablation in terms of accuracy and speed.**

Index Terms*—*Autonomous Catheterization; Finite Element Analysis; Steerable Catheter; Radio Frequency Ablation; Parametric Simulation.

I. Introduction

In the elderly population, Atrial Fibrillation (AFib) is the most common arrhythmia, in which the electrical activity within the atria becomes chaotic [1]. Consequently, chaotic contractions of the atrium may result in blood clots and strokes [2]. As a treatment, in Radio Frequency Ablation (RFA), the arrhythmogenic sites within the cardiac tissue are partially burned off to reduce the undesired pulsation within the cardiac tissue. Catheters are thin tubes made of medical-grade materials that are inserted through small incisions into the body. The majority of atrial ablation procedures are carried out using manual catheters; however, robotic catheter intervention systems have been introduced to enable more precise mapping and ablation procedures [3][4]. It has been shown that excessive contact force (greater than 0.45 N) increases the incidence of tissue perforation, while inadequate force (less than 0.1 N) results in ineffective ablation. Figure 1 shows a scheme of a cardiac steerable RFA catheter used for AFib treatment. For RFA catheters, researchers have proposed

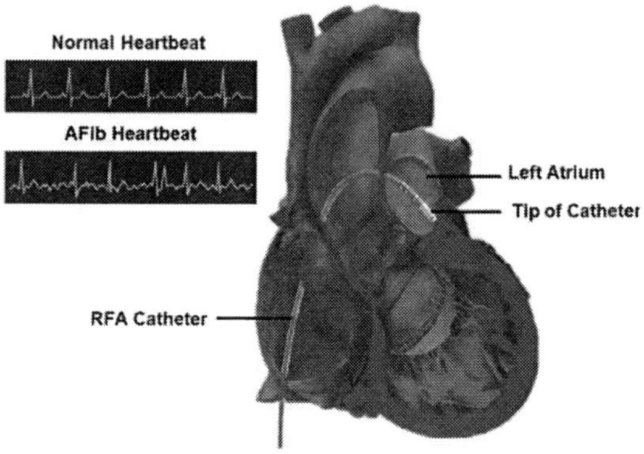

Fig. 1. Configuration of a typical ablation's catheter during an RFA procedure and a comparison of normal and arrhythmic cardiac electrical activity. (3D Heart model from Zygote Media Group Inc.)

sensor-based [5][6], and model-based [3] shape estimation schemes [7]. Even though sensor-based studies have shown favorable accuracy [8][9][10], sensor-embedded catheters are limited by their size, weight, compromised flexibility, and high cost [11]. In the literature, sensor-free approaches for estimating force have been proposed based on shape sensing [12]. Typically, these methods use real-time images of a deflected catheter to determine tip contact forces based on a mechanistic model of the catheter. Among the mechanistic methods to model the catheter is the Pseudo-Rigid-Body (PRB) model, which showed low accuracy [13][14] to be used in the medical applications. Also, the other models such as interaction modeling [15], piecewise circular arcs [16], spatial curves [17], Kirchhoff models [18], and Cosserat rod models [19][20], are not suitable for estimating the shape of the catheter in real-time because they are mainly computationally expensive. On the other hand, learning-based methods have been proposed to estimate the contact forces directly from the images containing the deflection shapes of the distal shaft [21] [22]. However, such approaches are in need to be fed by the realistic data obtained from experimental setups. Compiling a dataset that comprises all possible deflections with respect

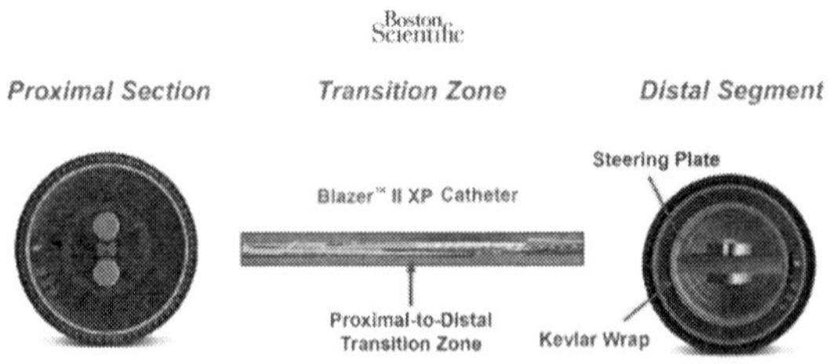

Fig. 2. Cross-section of the steerable catheter, Blazer II XP, Model 4770THK2, Boston Scientific [23].

to the eclectic catheter's material is costly and cumbersome. The scientific achievement of this study is the development of a real-time force estimator for robot-assisted radio frequency ablation using finite element analysis.

Given the reviewed limitations, this study proposes a parametric Finite Element Model (FEM) to simulate the deformation of a steerable catheter and estimate the tip contact force. The main contribution of this study is to propose a shape-based force estimation according to the finite element simulation. Due to the availability of real-time X-ray images during RFA procedures (fluoroscopy), the shape of the RFA catheter is available intraoperatively. Given such a capability, the proposed simulation can pave the way for leveraging the deep learning potentiality in finding the relationship between the parameters and their corresponding bending shape. This will obviate the run-time issue in the simulation-based approaches. Having a precise shape of the catheter along with the generated contact force outputted by the proposed simulation, it will also be possible to estimate the contact forces using the proposed method by matching the authentic catheter's deflection to the simulation output. Section II describes the finite element model used in this study. In Section III, validation of the simulation using the experimental setup will be presented and the results of the model are shown in Section IV. Finlay, the main contributions of this study will be concluded in Section V.

II. Finite Element Simulation

In this study, the catheter is modeled as a cantilever beam with a length of $L = 108$ mm and diameter $D = 2.33$ mm (this size is equivalent to the French size 7). These are the dimensions of the available catheter (Blazer II XP, Model 4770THK2, total length 110 cm, Boston Scientific [23]). Only the distal segment of the catheter was imported into the simulation. Figure 2 shows the cross-section of the proximal section and distal segment of the catheter. Since different materials are used to prototype the catheter (e.g., kevlar wrap and steering plate), the equivalent Young's modulus, Poisson's ratio and density are considered as parameters in the finite element simulations of the catheter. Then based on the deformation of the catheter during the experimental setup, the values for these parameters are tuned. During the simulation, the catheter's tip was squeezed on a rigid surface (e.g., the lumens or cardiac tissues) for 40 mm, and the reaction force at the base was recorded. Figure 3 shows the FE homogeneous Dirichlet and

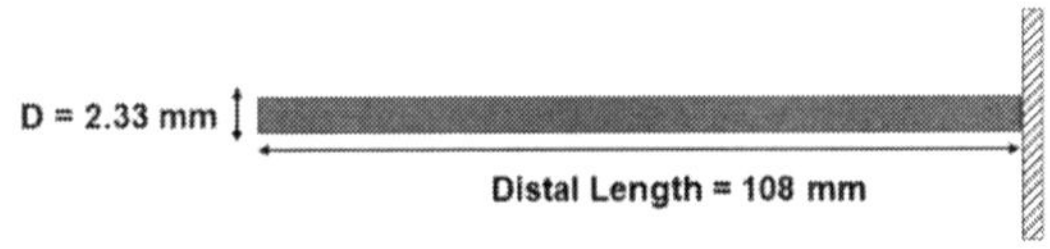

Fig. 3. Cantilever condition for the distal shaft of the catheter.

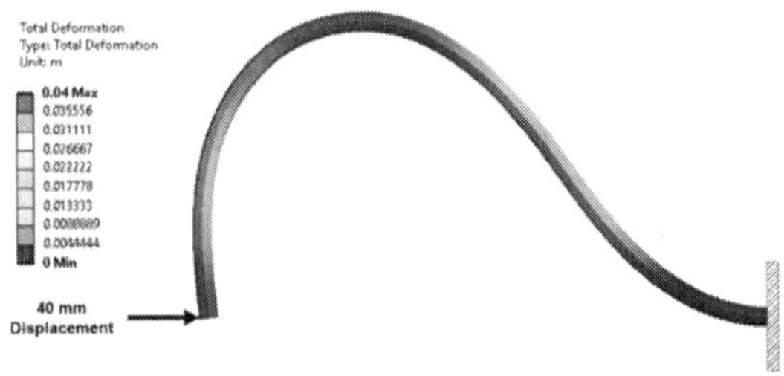

Fig. 4. Deformed shape of the catheter under 40 mm tip displacement.

Neumann boundary conditions which were applied at the rightmost of the model to simulate the cantilever condition for the distal shaft of the catheter. The model was discretized and solved using 108 elements and the nonlinear geometry (large deformation) assumption using ANSYS software (ANSYS Inc., PA, USA). Figure 4 shows the representative deformed shape of the catheter under 40 mm tip displacement. Next section will provide more details of the simulations validation.

III. Validation Study

To validate the parametric simulation and find the material properties, a range for every three parameters is considered as follows: Young's modulus ranges from 120 to 200 MPa, Poisson's ratio from 0.3 to 0.4, and density from 7000 to 8000 kg/m^3. The range specifies the minimum and maximum of each parameter during the simulation. Table I shows the experimental points for the range of each parameter and the corresponding reaction force.

TABLE I
Parametric Study Experiment Points

Experiment Points	Density (kg/m^3)	Young's Modulus (MPa)	Poisson Ratio	Reaction Force (N)
1	7500	160	0.35	0.4882
2	7000	160	0.35	0.4881
3	8000	160	0.35	0.4884
4	7500	120	0.35	0.3669
5	7500	200	0.35	0.6096
6	7500	160	0.3	0.4883
7	7500	160	0.4	0.4882
8	7093.48	127.47	0.31	0.3895
9	7906.51	127.47	0.31	0.3898
10	7093.48	192.52	0.31	0.5868
11	7906.51	192.52	0.31	0.5871
12	7093.48	127.47	0.39	0.3894
13	7906.51	127.47	0.39	0.3897
14	7093.48	192.52	0.39	0.5867
15	7906.51	192.52	0.39	0.5870

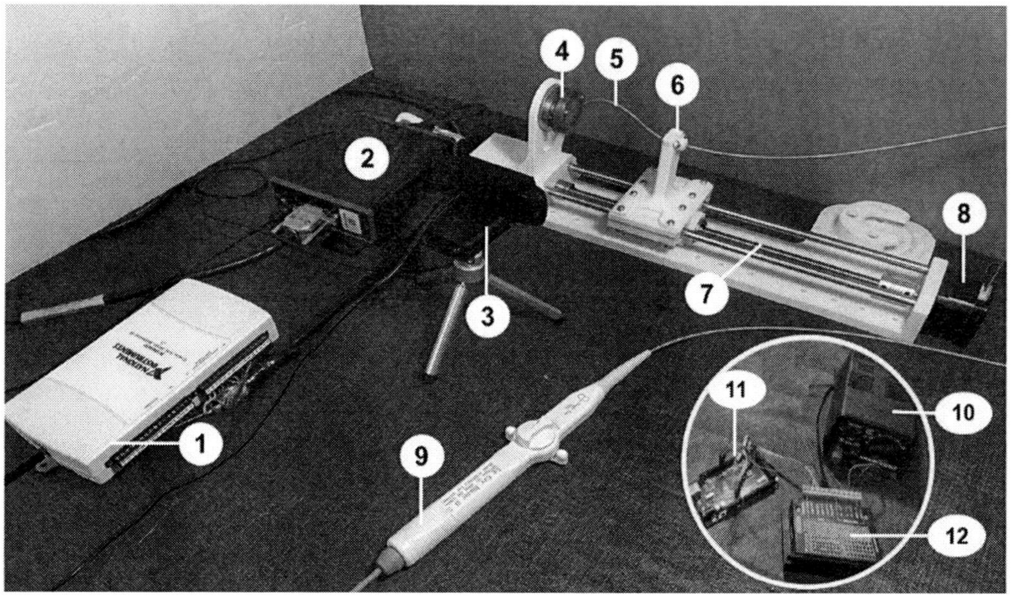

Fig. 5. Experimental setup, (1) data acquisition unit [24] (2) power supply of sensor [24] (3) camera (4) ATI Industrial Automation, F/T Sensor: Mini40 [24] (5) tip of the catheter (6) holder (7) linear actuator (8) Nema 17 stepper motor (9) steerable catheter, Blazer II XP, Model 4770THK2, Boston Scientific [23] (10) power supply (11) Arduino MEGA 2560 (12) microstep driver.

The experimental setup in Figure 5 mimics the catheter simulation. Prior to the experiment, 108 mm length of the catheter tip was measured and fixed in the holder of the linear actuator. The linear actuator was rapidly prototyped using a 3D printer (Replicator+, MakerBot, NY, USA) so as to align the center of the holder and 6-DoF force/torque sensor (ATI Industrial Automation, F/T Sensor: Mini40) (Figure 5 (4)) [24]. The purpose of the 6-DoF force/torque sensor is to measure the force applied to the clamped base by the tip of the catheter. Next, a Nema 17 stepper motor (Figure 5 (8)) controlled by an Arduino MEGA 2560 (Figure 5 (11)) squeezed the catheter tip against the force sensor mounted at the end of the linear actuator. It is the purpose of the stepper motor to drive the linear actuator. Simultaneously, a camera (Figure 5 (3)) perpendicular to the deflection plane was used to record the deflection of the catheter. During the experiment, the catheter tip's bending angle was set to 0° by using the catheter's knob, and also the initial shape of the catheter was straight. The wiring of the stepper motor in Figure 5 (8) is connected microstep driver Figure 5 (12). Figure 6 compares the result of the experiment and simulation when the tip of the catheter was squeezed for 40 mm. Utilizing ANSYS's response surface optimization (RSO) module, the candidate point is selected with the aim of minimizing the error between the reaction force obtained from the force sensor and the simulation. Figure 7 shows the recorded force during the experiment. Next section provides the result and discussion of the study.

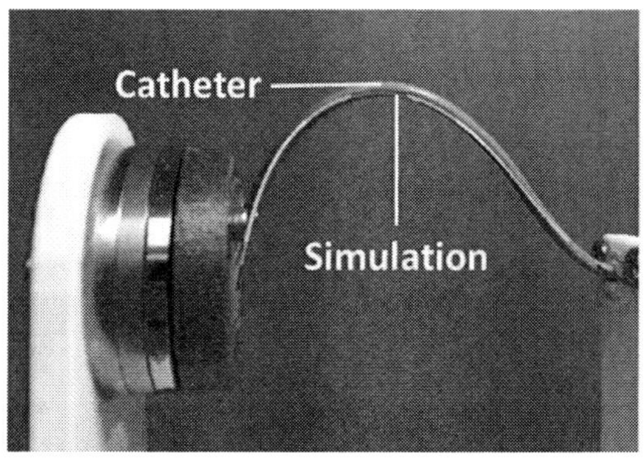

Fig. 6. Comparison of FEM simulation and experimental deformation for the tip of catheter when the catheter squeezed 40 mm to the force sensor.

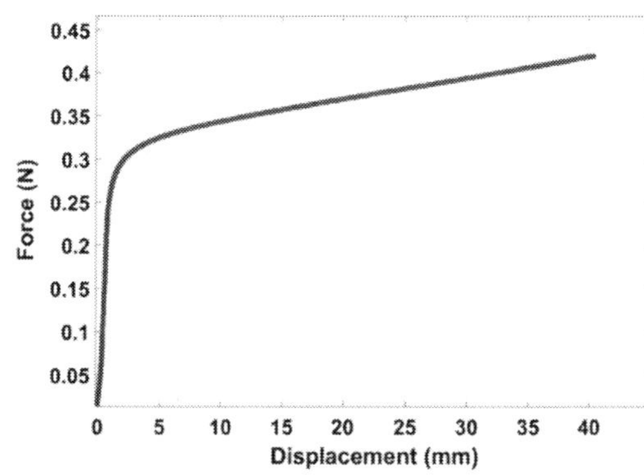

Fig. 7. Recorded force during the experiment when the tip of the catheter was squeezed for 40 mm.

IV. Result And Discussion

Table II shows the candidate values for the Young's modulus, Poisson ratio and density of the catheter found using

TABLE II
MECHANICAL PROPERTIES OF CATHETER FOUND USING THE RSO.

Young's modulus (MPa)	Poisson ratio	Density (kg/m^3)
137.6	0.394	7736

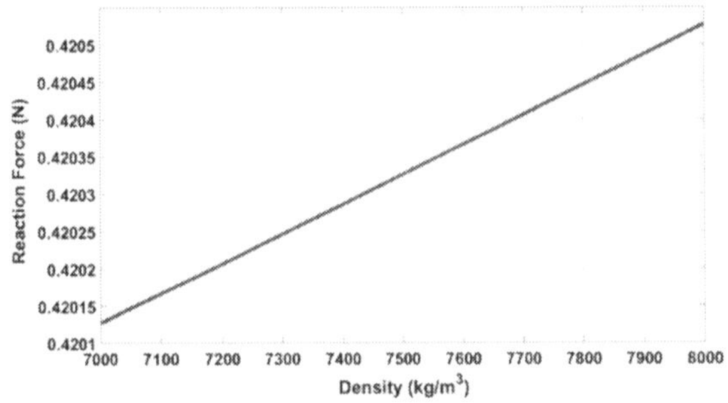

Fig. 8. Variation of reaction force by changing the density in the range of 7000 to 8000 (kg/m^3) while Young's modulus and Poisson's ratio are set to candidate values.

the RSO. The candidate points are the selected values of Young's modulus, Poisson's ratio, and density from I that satisfied the 0.4 N reaction force with 40 mm tip displacement. Figure 8 shows the variation of reaction force by changing the density in the range of 7000 to 8000 (kg/m^3) while Young's modulus and Poisson's ratio are set to 137.6 MPa and 0.394, respectively. Similarly, Figure 9 and Figure 10 show the variation of reaction force by changing the Young's modulus and Poisson ratio while other parameters are set to the candidate values. The Figures showed the sensitivity of the reaction force to the Young's modulus and Poisson ratio.

As illustrated in Figures 8 and 10, the reaction force is slightly changed by the variation of the density and Poisson's ratio. However, as shown in Figure 9 the reaction force is highly dependent on the value of Young's modulus. In addition, igures 11 to 13 provide a 3D plot of the variation in reaction force at the selected candidate points. The results showed that the reaction force increased by incensing Young's modulus and density. The reason for this is that the capability

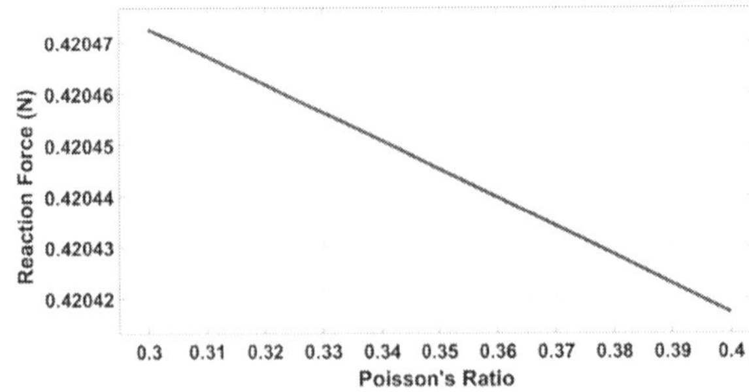

Fig. 10. Variation of reaction force by changing the Poisson's ratio in the range of 0.3 to 0.4 while Young's modulus and density are set to candidate values.

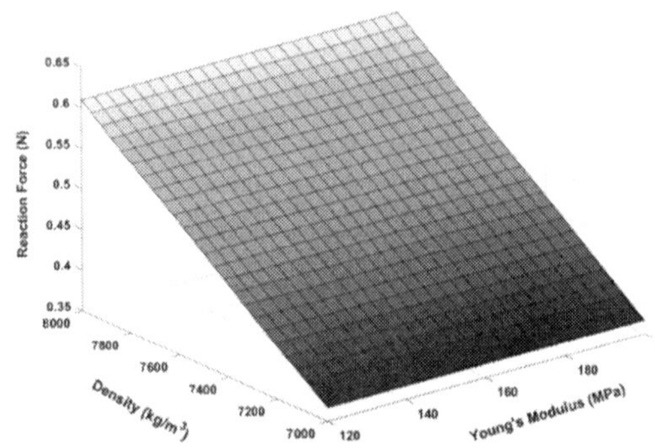

Fig. 11. Variation of reaction force by changing the Young's modulus and density.

of transferring force is directly related to the material property, and that by increasing the material property and having a stiffer material, more force can be transferred. However, by increasing the Poisson's ratio, the reaction force decreased. Moreover, as the catheter's tip weight is small, density almost has no impact on the reaction force, proving the validity of the quasi-statistics assumption in the FEM modeling and in the applications that the velocity of deformation is slow.

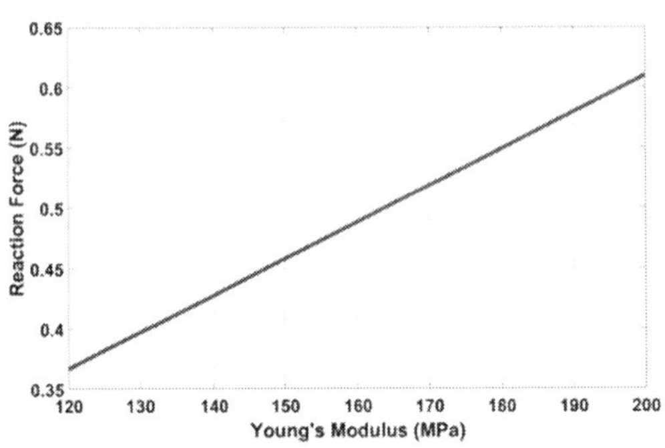

Fig. 9. Variation of reaction force by changing the Young's modulus in the range of 120 to 200 MPa while density and Poisson's ratio are set to candidate values.

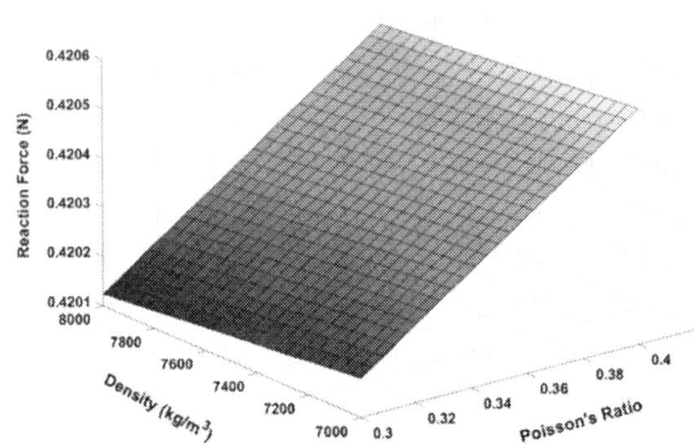

Fig. 12. Variation of reaction force by changing the Poisson's ratio and density.

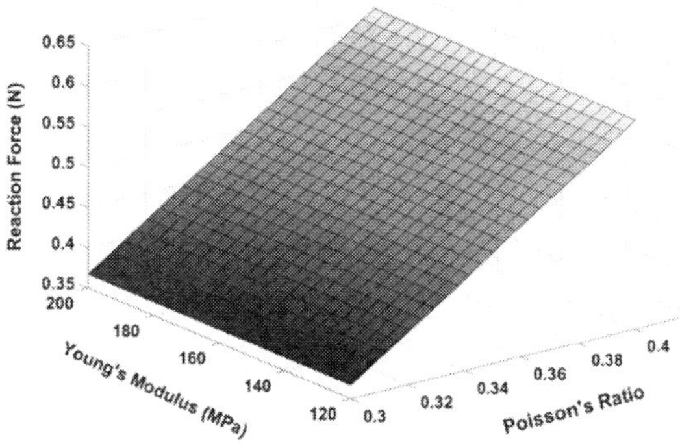

Fig. 13. Variation of reaction force by changing the Poisson's ratio and Young's modulus.

V. Conclusion And Future Work

A real-time force estimator is necessary for ensuring the safety and effectiveness of robot-assisted radio frequency ablation. The purpose of this study was to simulate a parametric finite element model for a steerable catheter which will be used for the estimation of force during radio frequency ablation procedures. A setup experiment is conducted to determine the design parameters of the catheter by comparing the deformation of the catheter between the experiment (by capturing the deformation of the catheter) and the finite element simulations. The results of the FE simulation were in fair agreement with the reference values obtained from the experiment. Based on the outcome of the current study, the proposed method was able to meet both the accuracy and speed requirements for procedures involving robot-assisted autonomous cardiac ablation. In terms of simulation speed, the time required for the ablation process to be completed can be measured and compared against a desired time frame or benchmark. For future work, a learning-from-simulation model will be proposed to estimate the tip contact force without actually running the simulation in real-time. This feature will enhance the accuracy and precision of minimally invasive procedures for robotic catheter intervention systems.

Acknowledgment

This research was supported by the Natural Science and Engineering Research Council (NSERC) of Canada through the NSERC CREATE Grant for Innovation-at-the-Cutting-Edge (ICE), the Fonds de Recherche du Quebec pour la Nature et les Technologies (FRQNT), Concordia University, and McGill University, Montreal, Quebec, Canada.

References

[1] G. F. Romiti et al., "Adherence to the 'atrial fibrillation better care'pathway in patients with atrial fibrillation: impact on clinical outcomes—a systematic review and meta-analysis of 285,000 patients," Thrombosis and haemostasis, vol. 122, no. 03, pp. 406–414, 2022.

[2] K. G. Graves et al., "Atrial fibrillation ablation and its impact on stroke," Current treatment options in cardiovascular medicine, vol. 20, no. 1, pp. 1–12, 2018.

[3] A. Hooshiar, S. Najarian, and J. Dargahi, "Haptic telerobotic cardiovascular intervention: a review of approaches, methods, and future perspectives," IEEE reviews in biomedical engineering, vol. 13, pp. 32–50, 2019.

[4] M. Runciman, A. Darzi, and G. P. Mylonas, "Soft robotics in minimally invasive surgery," Soft robotics, vol. 6, no. 4, pp. 423–443, 2019.

[5] N. Bandari, J. Dargahi, and M. Packirisamy, "Tactile sensors for minimally invasive surgery: A review of the state-of-the-art, applications, and perspectives," Ieee Access, vol. 8, pp. 7682–7708, 2019.

[6] N. M. Bandari, A. Hooshair, M. Packirisamy, and J. Dargahi, "Optical fiber array sensor for lateral and circumferential force measurement suitable for minimally invasive surgery: Design, modeling and analysis," in Specialty Optical Fibers. Optica Publishing Group, 2016.

[7] A. Sayadi, H. R. Nourani, M. Jolaei, J. Dargahi, and A. Hooshiar, "Force estimation on steerable catheters through learning-from-simulation with ex-vivo validation," in 2021 International Symposium on Medical Robotics (ISMR). IEEE, 2021, pp. 1–6.

[8] T. Torkaman, M. Roshanfar, J. Dargahi, and A. Hooshiar, "Embedded six-dof force-torque sensor for soft robots with learning-based calibration," IEEE Sensors Journal, 2023.

[9] T. Torkaman, M. Roshanfar, J. Dargahi, and A. Hooshiar, "Accurate embedded force sensor for soft robots with rate-dependent deep neural calibration," in 2022 IEEE International Symposium on Robotic and Sensors Environments (ROSE). IEEE, 2022, pp. 1–7.

[10] T. Torkaman, M. Roshanfar, J. Dargahi, and A. Hooshiar, "Analytical modeling and experimental validation of a gelatin-based shape sensor for soft robots," in 2022 International Symposium on Medical Robotics (ISMR). IEEE, 2022, pp. 1–7.

[11] L. Zou, C. Ge, Z. J. Wang, E. Cretu, and X. Li, "Novel tactile sensor technology and smart tactile sensing systems: A review," Sensors, vol. 17, no. 11, p. 2653, 2017.

[12] A. Hooshiar, N. M. Bandari, and J. Dargahi, "Image-based estimation of contact forces on catheters for robot-assisted cardiovascular intervention," in Hamlyn Symposium on Medical Robotics, 2018, pp. 119–120.

[13] M. Khoshnam and R. V. Patel, "Estimating contact force for steerable ablation catheters based on shape analysis," in 2014 IEEE/RSJ International Conference on Intelligent Robots and Systems. IEEE, 2014, pp. 3509–3514.

[14] A. Molaei, A. G. Aghdam, and J. Dargahi, "A versatile pseudo-rigid body modeling method," arXiv preprint arXiv:2206.06237, 2022.

[15] M. Jolaeimoghaddam, S. A. H. Ahmedi, and J. Dargahi, "Sensor-free force and position control of tendon-driven catheters through interaction modeling," Jul. 14 2022, uS Patent App. 17/647,673.

[16] S. Hasanzadeh and F. Janabi-Sharifi, "Model-based force estimation for intracardiac catheters," IEEE/ASME Transactions on Mechatronics, vol. 21, no. 1, pp. 154–162, 2015.

[17] M. Jolaei, A. Hooshiar, J. Dargahi, and M. Packirisamy, "Toward task autonomy in robotic cardiac ablation: Learning-based kinematic control of soft tendon-driven catheters," Soft Robotics, vol. 8, no. 3, pp. 340–351, 2021.

[18] M. Luo, H. Xie, L. Xie, P. Cai, and L. Gu, "A robust and real-time vascular intervention simulation based on kirchhoff elastic rod," Computerized medical imaging and graphics, vol. 38, no. 8, pp. 735–743, 2014.

[19] M. Roshanfar, A. Sayadi, J. Dargahi, and A. Hooshiar, "Stiffness adaptation of a hybrid soft surgical robot for improved safety in interventional surgery," in 2022 44th Annual International Conference of the IEEE Engineering in Medicine & Biology Society (EMBC). IEEE, 2022, pp. 4853–4859.

[20] M. Roshanfar, J. Dargahi, and A. Hooshiar, "Toward semi-autonomous stiffness adaptation of pneumatic soft robots: Modeling and validation," in 2021 IEEE International Conference on Autonomous Systems (ICAS). IEEE, 2021, pp. 1–5.

[21] P. Fekri et al., "Y-net: A deep convolutional architecture for 3d estimation of contact forces in intracardiac catheters," IEEE Robotics and Automation Letters, vol. 7, no. 2, pp. 3592–3599, 2022.

[22] P. Fekri et al., "A deep learning force estimator system for intracardiac catheters," 2021 IEEE International Symposium on Medical Measurements and Applications (MeMeA), vol. 7, no. 2, pp. 1–6, 2021.

[23] Boston Scientific, "Blazer XP temperature ablation catheter family," shorturl.at/bpszM, 2023.

[24] ATI Industrial Automation, "ATI multi-axis force/torque sensor, mini40," shorturl.at/bDKSZ, 2023.

Multi-Agent Planning Method Using Affordances from Environment

Sawako Tajima
Graduate School of Sci. and Tech.
Keio University
Yokohama, Kanagawa, Japan
email: sawako_tajima_0727@keio.jp

Daiki Takamura
Graduate School of Sci.and Tech.
Keio University
Yokohama, Kanagawa, Japan
email: d.takamura.1102@keio.jp

Daiki Shimokawa
Graduate School of Sci. and Tech.
Keio University
Yokohama, Kanagawa, Japan
email: jump1204@keio.jp

Reo Kobayashi
Graduate School of Sci. and Tech.
Keio University
Yokohama, Kanagawa, Japan
email: reokoba@keio.jp

Reo Abe
Faculty of Sci. and Tech.
Keio University
Yokohama, Kanagawa, Japan
email: reo1431@keio.jp

Satoshi Kurihara
Faculty of Sci. and Tech.
Keio University
Yokohama, Kanagawa, Japan
email: satoshi@keio.jp

Abstract—**For autonomous actors, such as robots to achieve their goals while operating adaptively in a dynamically changing environment, they need to accurately recognize changing conditions from moment to moment. Planning research for finding a sequence of actions to achieve a goal has a long history, and in recent years, machine learning has become the mainstream method for finding the optimal sequence of actions. However, it is difficult to deal with unexpected situations using this method, and in such cases, the real-time performance is lost due to the blind search for a sequence of actions that will achieve the goal. Living organisms, such as ourselves, have learned how to avoid blind search by perceiving environmental affordances. In this paper, we propose a method for robots to use affordances to recognize their situation accurately and to seek a sequence of actions to achieve their goals efficiently. Affordances are common sense in an individual situation, i.e., tacit knowledge, and conventionally can only be constructed manually, which has the limitation that they cannot be scaled. However, large-scale language models that have recently emerged may contain tacit knowledge, and we have developed a method for extracting this tacit knowledge. In this study, we incorporated this method into a multi-agent planning system that is highly adaptive to dynamic environmental changes. We confirmed that a sequence of actions can be efficiently obtained to achieve a goal by using affordances.**

Keywords—multi-agent planning; action selection; affordance.

I. INTRODUCTION

Planning is an essential area of Artificial Intelligence (AI) research and continues to be actively studied. In particular, planning, which is highly adaptive to dynamic environments, is a core technology for realizing next-generation AI with high autonomy and versatility.

To realize this capability, it is necessary to distinguish between immediate planning, which enables instantaneous action selection in response to changes in the environment, and deliberative planning, which outputs a highly optimal action sequence even if it takes time to achieve a goal that requires deliberation, given to a robot equipped with the planning system.

A method to construct the planner as a multi-agent type has been proposed to achieve immediacy and deliberateness. In multi-agent planning, one agent is in charge of one operant in Stanford Research Institute Problem Solver (STRIPS) [1], and the agents cooperate to generate a sequence of operants that transitions from the initial state to the goal state. Subsumption Architecture (SA) proposed by Brooks [2] is well known as an existing study. SA can hierarchically connect lower-level reflective functional modules and higher-level deliberative functional modules to use immediacy and deliberateness as appropriate. However, SA exclusively selects between immediate and deliberative planning, and the two cannot cooperate or be more adaptive to the environment.

On the other hand, Agent Network Architecture (ANA) proposed by Maes [3] [4] is an activation propagation-based behavioral network architecture. This method allows more fine-grained coordination between immediate response and deliberation than SA by allowing agents to interact with each other in the form of activation propagation.

However, in planning, a search is conducted to obtain action sequences, and the more versatile the planning is, the more the search for the optimal sequence that achieves the objective from among a vast number of combinations of action sequences becomes burdensome and real-time performance declines. In planning, many methods have been proposed in recent years to find the optimal action sequence by machine learning. However, even with this method, unexpected situations are difficult to deal with. In such cases, blind search is achieved for a sequence of actions that achieves the objective, which results in a loss of real-time performance.

Living organisms, such as ourselves, can avoid blind search by perceiving environmental affordances. Affordance is 'the opportunity for action that an organism receives from a particular object or environment' [5]. For example, if a human perceives a door with a handle, he/she can obtain the affordance of pulling from this door to open it. Affordances are common sense in an individual situation, i.e., tacit knowledge, and conventionally can only be constructed manually, which has the limitation that they cannot be scaled.

However, we believe large-scale language models that have recently emerged may contain tacit knowledge. If this can

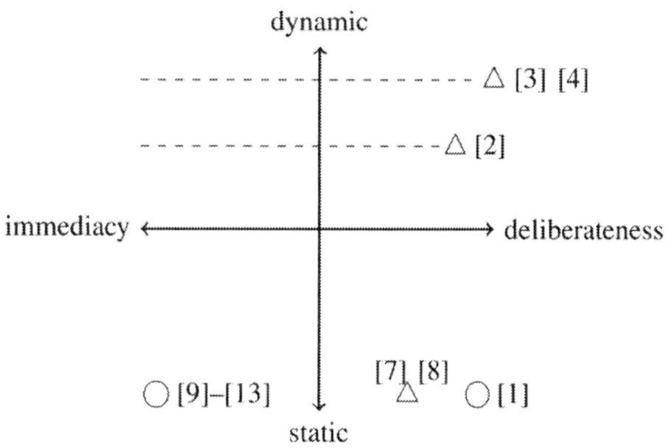

Figure 1. Comparison of related works.

be automatically extracted, affordances can be easily used. Our research aims to incorporate affordances into multi-agent planning and use affordances to obtain a sequence of actions to achieve a goal efficiently.

Naturally, robots cannot receive affordances from the environment, so common sense and tacit knowledge have needed to be manually set for each task given to the robot. Therefore, the greater the generality of planning, the greater the amount of tacit knowledge to be set, and the more difficult it becomes to set by hand.

To address this issue, we focus on large-scale language models such as Generative Pre-trained Transformer 3 (GPT-3) [6] that have recently emerged. Since this model was constructed by learning a huge amount of linguistic information, it can be said to contain tacit knowledge and common sense. In this study, we propose a method for automatically extracting affordances from this large-scale language model in accordance with the situation and using them for planning. The proposed method enables the robot to understand the dynamically changing environment by understanding its situation and to plan adaptively to achieve its goals while avoiding unnecessary searches for sequences of actions.

In Section 2, we compare related works in planning, and in Section 3, we introduce our proposed method. Section 4 describes the evaluation conducted to confirm the significance of the proposed method, and Section 5 describes the results and the discussion. Finally, Section 6 presents the conclusion and future work.

II. Related Work

In this section, we present related work in planning. Figure 1 plots each method based on the characteristics. The horizontal axis in the figure represents immediacy and deliberateness, and the vertical axis represents the ability to adapt to a dynamic environment. The plotted symbols are marked ○ for methods that take a long time but output an optimal action sequence and △ for methods that output a suboptimal action sequence within a limited time (i.e., with "anytime" property).

The most typical method of classical planning is STRIPS [1]. STRIPS outputs a sequence of actions to transform an initial state into a goal state. Although STRIPS can output an optimal action sequence, it is problematic because it requires a significant amount of time for search. Research to improve the efficiency of the search is still ongoing. Shen et al. [7] introduced the concept of hypergraphs to output a suboptimal action sequence in a limited amount of time. Domshlak et al. [8] detected state symmetries within A* cost-optimal planning, allowing them to prune a larger portion of the search space. However, these methods are difficult to adapt to dynamic environments because they require planning to be redone from scratch when the environment changes, which is computationally very expensive.

In recent years, machine learning has been actively used to find optimal action sequences. Many methods have been proposed in deep reinforcement learning based on DQN [14], such as Rainbow [9], APE-X [10], R2D2 [11], and NGU [12]. In particular, Badia et al. [13] have outperformed standard human performance on all Atari games. The advantages of such machine learning-based methods are that they can automatically extract features from large amounts of observed data and achieve high accuracy in the environment and task for which they were trained. However, because learning is based on observed data, they are not good at dealing with dynamic environments, such as changing the priority of tasks in accordance with changes in the environment when there are multiple objectives. Therefore, learning priorities by considering the immediacy and deliberateness of multiple objectives in every situation is not practical because the learning load is too high.

A further method is to construct the planner as a multi-agent type. In a Multi-Agent Planner (MAP), each agent is responsible for an individual operant in STRIPS [1] and generates a sequence of operants that transition from the initial state to the target state through agent coordination. SA [2] can connect lower-level reflective functional modules and higher-level deliberative functional modules hierarchically to use immediacy and deliberateness as appropriate. However, SA exclusively selects between immediate and deliberative planning, and the two cannot cooperate or be more adaptive to the environment. Maes [3] [4] proposed an activation-propagating Agent Network Architecture (ANA). In ANA, an agent will attempt to act if the state of the environment matches the conditions under which it will act. Each goal of the robot tries to activate an agent to achieve it, and the agent in turn tries to activate another agent to activate itself further. Therefore, ANA can use immediacy and deliberateness more flexibly than SA by allowing agents to interact in activation propagation. However, ANA has the disadvantage of requiring manually designed agents, making it difficult to scale. MAP continues to be studied today, with research using ANA to make conversational decisions with users [15] and research combining state-based and action-based frameworks to control dynamic behavior [16]. There are also studies using multi-agents for natural disaster modeling [17] and inventory modeling [18] to increase prediction accuracy while reducing reliance on the experience of experts. Thus, although MAP is

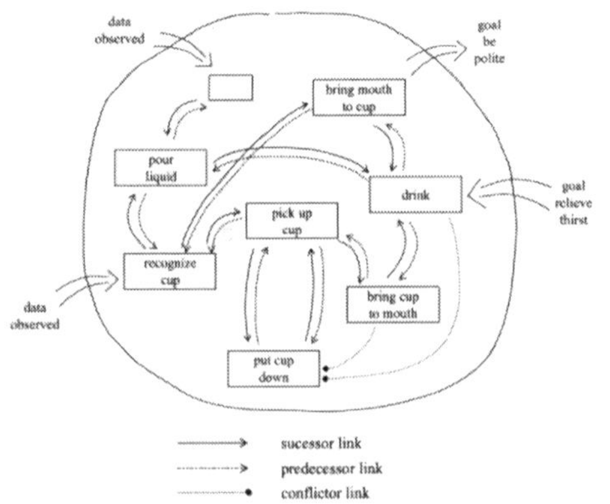

Figure 2. The network of ANA [3].

inferior to other methods in terms of optimality, it is superior at responding to dynamic environments.

III. Proposed Method

We consider that using affordances can solve the disadvantage of the MAP. Humans similarly use affordances to reduce the search space, reducing the brain's load. This is the inspiration for the proposed method. In this study, we propose extending the MAP method that utilizes affordance information. We also propose a method for extracting affordance information from large-scale language models.

A. Agent Network Architecture (ANA)

In this paper, ANA [3] [4] is used as the baseline for MAP because ANA can use immediacy and deliberateness flexibly. This section describes the architecture of the ANA and the algorithm for action selection.

ANA has agents equivalent to STRIPS [1] operants and consists of a network connecting them. Each agent has a condition list, add list, and delete list. The condition list contains states necessary for execution, the add list contains states to be added to the current environment after execution, and the delete list contains states to be deleted from the current environment.

Figure 2 shows the ANA network, consisting of a network of agents connected to each other by three links: predecessor, successor, and conflictor. A predecessor link is a link between two agents when an agent satisfies the preconditions of an agent (has a condition list state in the add-list). A successor link is a link between two agents when there is an agent that can be executed after the execution of an agent (has an add list state in the condition list). A conflictor link is a link between two agents when an agent becomes non-executable (has a condition list state in the delete list) after an agent is executed.

Through these links, activation propagation from the environment, goal, and protected goal (external spreading) and activation propagation between agents (internal spreading) are performed. The amount of stimulus accumulated by activation propagation is called the activation level. Each agent has a threshold, the minimum activation level required for activation. The agent is activated and executed when the activation level exceeds the threshold. This sequence of events is called selection. The agent that can be executed from the current environment is selected and executed by repeating the selection process. The following is a formula for the activation level of agent y at time t.

$$\begin{aligned}\alpha(y,t) = {} & decay(\alpha(y,t-1)(1-active(y,t-1)) \\ & + input\_from\_state(y,t) \\ & + input\_from\_goals(y,t) \\ & - taken\_away\_by\_protected\_goals(y,t) \\ & + \sum_{x,z}(spreads\_bw(x,y,t) \\ & \quad + spreads\_fw(x,y,t) \\ & \quad - takes\_away(z,y,t)))\end{aligned} \quad (1)$$

The $decay()$ that runs throughout (1) is a function that normalizes the activation level of all agents in the network. $\alpha(y,t-1)(1-active(y,t-1))$ in the first line indicates whether the activation level of agent y at time $t-1$ is used at time t. The agent active at time $t-1$ is calculated with $active(y,t-1)=1$, and the agent not active at time t is calculated with $active(y,t-1)=0$.

The parameters used in the formulas after the second line of (1) are shown below.

- ϕ, the amount of activation energy injected by the state per true proposition
- γ, the amount of activation energy injected by the goals per goal
- δ, the amount of activation energy taken away by the protected goals per protected goal
- $S(t)$, the set of states that are true at time t
- $M(j)$, the set of agents with state j in condition list
- $A(j)$, the set of agents with state j in add list
- $U(j)$, the set of agents with state j in delete list
- c_y, condition list of agent y
- a_y, add list of agent y
- d_y, delete list of agent y

The second line of (1) represents the amount of stimuli that agent y receives from the environment, which is calculated by the following equation. In (2), # represents the size of the set or list.

$$input\_from\_state(y,t) = \sum_j \phi \frac{1}{\#M(j)} \frac{1}{\#c_y} \quad (2)$$

The third line of (1) represents the amount of stimulus that agent y receives from the goal and is calculated by the following equation.

$$input\_from\_goals(y,t) = \sum_j \gamma \frac{1}{\#A(j)} \frac{1}{\#a_y} \quad (3)$$

The fourth line of (1) represents the amount of stimuli that agent y receives from the protected goal, which is calculated by the following equation. Protected goal refers to a goal that has already been achieved or should be protected.

$$\begin{aligned} &taken\_away\_by\_protected\_goals(y,t) \\ &= \sum_j \delta \frac{1}{\#U(j)} \frac{1}{\#d_y} \end{aligned} \quad (4)$$

The fifth line of (1) represents the amount of stimuli sent from agent x to agent y via the predecessor link and is calculated by the following equation. If agent x is not executable at time t (the current environment does not satisfy the condition list of agent x), the stimulus is sent to agent y.

$$spreads\_bw(x,y,t) = \sum_j \alpha_x(t-1) \frac{1}{\#A(j)} \frac{1}{\#a_y} \quad (5)$$

The sixth line of (1) represents the amount of stimuli sent from the successor link from agent x to agent y, which is calculated by the following equation. If agent x is executable at time t (the current environment satisfies the condition list of agent x), then stimuli are sent to agent y.

$$spreads\_fw(x,y,t) = \sum_j \alpha_x(t-1) \frac{\phi}{\gamma} \frac{1}{\#M(j)} \frac{1}{\#c_y} \quad (6)$$

The seventh line of (1) represents the amount of stimuli sent from the conflictor link from agent z to agent y and is calculated by the following equation. Stimuli are sent to agent y when $\alpha_x(t-1) > \alpha_y(t-1) \vee (\exists i \notin S(t) \cap c_y \cap d_x)$ is satisfied.

$$\begin{aligned} &takes\_away(z,y,t) \\ &= max(\sum_j \alpha_x(t-1) \frac{\delta}{\gamma} \frac{1}{\#U(j)} \frac{1}{\#d_y}, \alpha_y(t-1)) \quad (7) \\ &where\, j \in c_x \cap d_y \cap S(t) \end{aligned}$$

B. Use of Affordances

Agents are expressed as a combination of a verb and a noun, as in "pick up cup", but it is common to describe a noun as a variable, as in "pick up X". In the MAP we are building, there are agents such as "wash X with Y (in right hand) in Z" (where X is the object, Y is the way, and Z is the location variable).

Since the noun "cup" affords verbs such as "drink", "grab by hand" and "wash" an agent such as "throw X" can be excluded from activation candidates from the beginning. However, if it does not use affordance, all verbs, including the object, must be considered candidates for activation.

Thus, if an agent such as "X" is "cup" and "pick up cup (on Z) with right hand" tries to activate it, it will have to consider all possible candidates for activation of Z if it does not use affordance. However, by using affordances, the agent can try

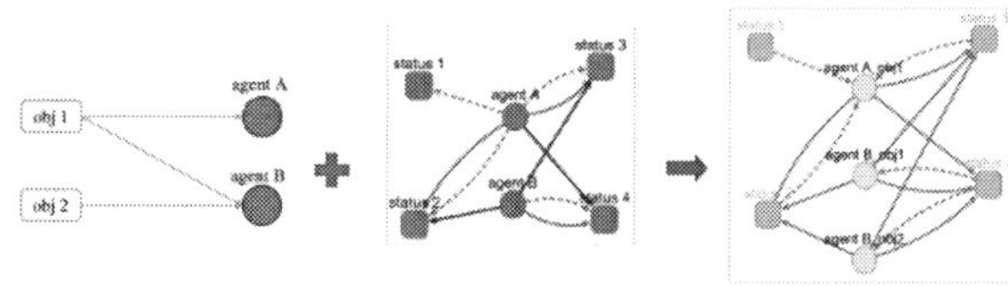

(a) Affordance Network (b) Variable Agent Behavior Network (c) Agent Behavior Network

Figure 3. The architecture of the proposed method.

to activate only those Zs that are appropriate to the situation, such as "table" or "rack", thus avoiding unnecessary search.

As described above, an agent containing variables such as X, Y, and Z is defined abstractly in advance, and actual concrete objects are assigned to the variable parts by using the affordance information described below. In this process, a generic agent with variables dynamically generates an agent representing each concrete action applicable to planning, and then planning is executed.

Figure 3 shows the architecture of the proposed method. Figure 3(a) shows Affordance Network, the network of objects and agents afforded by those objects connected by edges. Figure 3(b) shows Variable Agent Behavior Network, the MAP network of agents and states with noun parts as variables. Figure 3(c) shows Agent Behavior Network, MAP generated by connecting (a) and (b).

C. Affordance Extraction Methods

The sentences output from a large-scale language model such as GPT-3 express the knowledge contained in the large number of sentences humans have spun. In other words, outputting sentences related to a particular object is equivalent to outputting knowledge. In this study, we analyzed the output of the sentence by a large-scale language model grammatically. We call this network the affordance network.

An affordance network is constructed from a large-scale language model as follows.

1) Output sentences related to nouns using GPT-3.
2) Perform dependency parsing using CoreNLP [19] to extract dependency relations between verbs and nouns.
3) Build an affordance network from the extracted dependency relations.

In Step 1, GPT-3 outputs sentences using the following template of imperative sentences (prompts). By assigning the target nouns to {noun} in the prompt template, GPT-3 outputs a sentence containing knowledge about each noun. For example, a prompt with "cake" assigned to {noun} would produce a sentence like "He cut a cake with a knife."

- Please come up with some story.
  Keyword: {noun}
- Talk about your memories.
  Keyword: {noun}
- Please write a diary with yourself as the subject.
  Keyword: {noun}

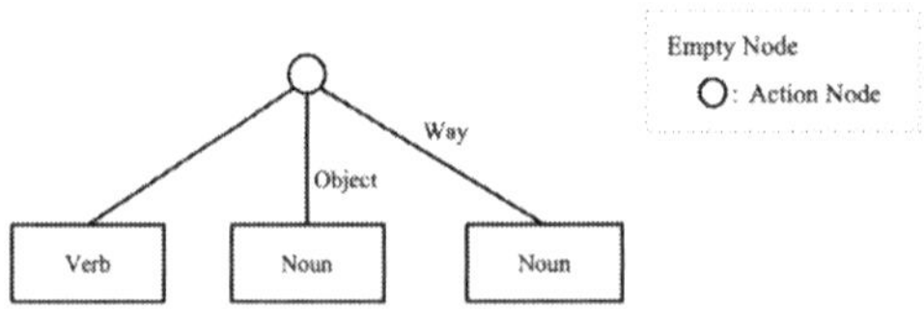

Figure 4. Affordance Network Structure.

In Step 2, the output of the sentence in Step 1 is subjected to dependency parsing using CoreNLP. By performing the dependency parsing, it is possible to identify the relationship between the verb and its object noun and the relationship between the verb and its way noun. For example, "cake" and "knife" are identified as the object and way of the verb "cut," respectively.

In Step 3, the network is constructed on the basis of the verb-noun affiliation relations identified in Step 2. Figure 4 shows the network.

IV. Evaluation

This section evaluates the introduction of the concept of affordance into MAP.

A. The Way to Use Affordance

Compared with SyntagNet [20], the proposed method better handles affordances inherent in the combination of multiple objects. For example, consider the output verb set V_{AB} when simultaneously observing object O_A and object O_B.

SyntagNet takes an object as input, outputs the verb set recalled from that object alone and outputs the verb sets V_A and V_B from O_A and O_B, respectively. On the other hand, the combination of O_A and O_B cannot directly be used to output a verb set, but only a union set $V_A \cup V_B$ or an intersection set $V_A \cap V_B$ can be given as an approximation of V_{AB}, for example.

The proposed method better outputs the set of verbs recalled when observing multiple objects simultaneously. The output of GPT-3, which has acquired a vast amount of human experience as knowledge, must include sentences that describe the experience of performing actions on one object using other objects as tools. In other words, GPT-3 also contains knowledge about actions specific to combinations of objects. Our proposed method is a networked output of GPT-3, which can directly output a set of verbs V_{AB} recalled for objects O_A and O_B.

Assume that SyntagNet outputs "cut" and "eat" from "apple", and "cut" and "stab" from "knife". The affordances of "apple" + "knife" would be defined as a union set ("cut", "eat", "stab") or an intersection set ("cut"). On the other hand, the proposed method can derive cut directly from the combination "apple" + "knife" rather than combining the affordances of individual objects.

B. Evaluation of MAP Incorporating Affordances

In this section, we built an ANA with built-in affordances and evaluated whether the proposed method can efficiently obtain a sequence of actions to achieve the goal.

TABLE I. COMPARISON OF RESULTS.

	With affordances	Without affordances
agent	16	90
link	73	346
activation propagation	273	1315

For this reason, we conducted experiments on simulations with and without the affordances extracted for ANA and compared them in terms of (a) the number of agents, (b) the number of links, and (c) the number of activation propagations required to achieve the goal. In (a), the greater the number of agents that do not contribute to activation for goal attainment, the more sure we can be that useless agents are provided. When useless agents are prepared, links are also prepared to connect them. Thus, in (b), the greater the number of links connecting the wasted agents, the more wasted activation propagation may occur. In (c), we counted the number of activation propagations until the goal set in the experiment was achieved. The smaller this number is, the more sure we can be that we can reduce the computational cost.

The experiment was conducted in a scenario that could occur in daily life, and the goal was to keep the windows clean. The scenario used two types of nouns (window, towel). The parameters in (1) were set to $\phi = 20, \gamma = 70, \delta = 50$ described in the original paper [4].

V. Discussion

a) The number of agents was 16 with affordances and 90 without affordances. In this experiment, only 6 agents contributed to the activation to achieve the goal, and most prepared agents were not used in the case of no affordances. Therefore, the with-affordance case is more efficient without unnecessarily activating many agents.

(b) The number of links was 73 with affordances and 346 without affordances. It can be seen that the number of links increased as the number of wasted agents was prepared in (a).

(c) From Table I, the number of activation propagations required to achieve the goal is clearly smaller in the case with affordances, thus reducing the computational cost. This result confirms that activation propagation is more compact and less wasteful with affordance.

Figure 5 compares agent behavior networks consisting of agents and links. The fact that the goal is achieved regardless of affordances confirms that appropriate action sequences can be obtained even with compact network configurations such as those with affordances.

VI. Conclusion and Future Work

In this paper, we proposed a method of automatically extracting affordances from a large-scale language model in accordance with the situation and using them in a MAP. The experiments demonstrated the effectiveness of using affordances, and we plan to address three points.

The first is to experiment in an unknown dynamic environment. This study conducted experiments in a known environment on the simulation. To verify the effectiveness of

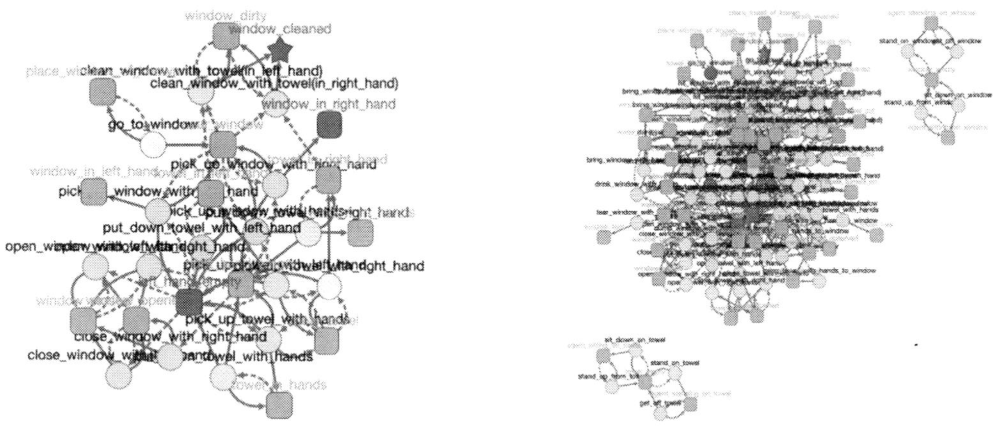

(a) With affordances

(b) Without affordances

Figure 5. Comparison of Agent Behavior Network.

the proposed MAP, its adaptability needs to be tested in a real-world, dynamically changing environment. In the future, we will test the MAP in a 3D simulation environment that simulates the real world.

The second point is to verify the object's affordance by considering its attributes. The organisms are able to associate the behavior of eating with red apples but not with brown apples. Thus, even for objects labeled with the same name, the fordable behavior should vary depending on attributes such as color, size, weight, shape, and texture. By considering the objects' attributes, we believe we can generate agents that are more appropriate to the situation.

The third point is to verify the results in several scenarios. The experiments conducted in this study were conducted under a single scenario. Experiments with several scenarios are necessary to verify the efficiency of the proposed method.

ACKNOWLEDGMENT

This work was supported by grant NEDO/Technology Development Project on Next-Generation Artificial Intelligence Evolving Together With Humans "Constructing Interactive Story-Type Contents Generation System".

REFERENCES

[1] R. E. Fikes and N. J. Nilsson, "STRIPS: A new approach to the application of theorem proving to problem solving," *Artificial Intelligence*, vol. 2, no. 3-4, pp. 189–208, 1971.

[2] R. Brooks, "A robust layered control system for a mobile robot," *IEEE Journal on Robotics and Automation*, vol. 2, no. 1, pp. 14–23, 1986.

[3] P. Maes, "The agent network architecture (ANA)," *ACM SIGART Bulletin*, vol. 2, no. 4, pp. 115–120, 1991.

[4] P. Maes, "How to do the right thing," *Connection science*, vol. 1, no. 3, pp. 291–323, 1989.

[5] J. J. Gibson, "The theory of affordances," *Hilldale, USA*, vol. 1, no. 2, pp. 67–82, 1977.

[6] T. Brown, B. Mann, N. Ryder, M. Subbiah, J. D. Kaplan *et al.*, "Language Models are Few-Shot Learners," *Advances in neural information processing systems*, vol. 33, pp. 1877–1901, 2020.

[7] W. Shen, F. Trevizan, and S. Thiébaux, "Learning domain-independent planning heuristics with hypergraph networks," *Proceedings of the International Conference on Automated Planning and Scheduling*, vol. 30, pp. 574–584, 2020.

[8] C. Domshlak, M. Katz, and A. Shleyfman, "Enhanced symmetry breaking in cost-optimal planning as forward search," in *Twenty-Second International Conference on Automated Planning and Scheduling*, 2012.

[9] M. Hessel, J. Modayil, H. V. Hasselt, T. Schaul, G. Ostrovski *et al.*, "Rainbow: combining improvements in deep reinforcement learning," in *Thirty-second AAAI conference on artificial intelligence*, vol. 32, 2018.

[10] D. Horgan, J. Quan, D. Budden, G. Barth-Maron, M. Hessel *et al.*, "Distributed prioritized experience replay," *arXiv*, 2018.

[11] S. Kapturowski, G. Ostrovski, J. Quan, R. Munos, and W. Dabney, "Recurrent experience replay in distributed reinforcement learning," in *International conference on learning representations*, 2019.

[12] A. P. Badia, P. Sprechmann, A. Vitvitskyi, D. Guo, B. Piot *et al.*, "Never give up: learning directed exploration strategies," *arXiv*, 2020.

[13] A. P. Badia, B. Piot, S. Kapturowski, P. Sprechmann, A. Vitvitskyi *et al.*, "Agent57: outperforming the atari human benchmark," in *International Conference on Machine Learning*, 2020, pp. 507–517.

[14] V. Mnih, K. Kavukcuoglu, D. Silver, A. Graves, I. Antonoglou *et al.*, "Playing Atari with deep reinforcement learning," *arXiv*, 2013.

[15] O. J. Romero, "Cognitively-inspired agent-based service composition for mobile and pervasive computing," in *International Conference on AI and Mobile Services*, 2019, pp. 101–117.

[16] P. Allgeuer and S. Behnke, "Hierarchical and state-based architectures for robot behavior planning and control," *arXiv*, 2018.

[17] J. Simmonds, J. A. Gómez, and A. Ledezma, "The role of agent-based modeling and multi-agent systems in flood-based hydrological problems: a brief review," *Journal of Water and Climate Change*, vol. 11, no. 4, pp. 1580–1602, 2020.

[18] J. H. Park and S. C. Park, "Agent-based merchandise management in business-to-business electronic commerce," *Decision Support Systems*, vol. 35, no. 3, pp. 311–333, 2003.

[19] C. Manning, M. Surdeanu, J. Bauer, J. Finkel, S. Bethard *et al.*, "The Stanford CoreNLP natural language processing toolkit," *Proceedings of 52nd Annual Meeting of the Association for Computational Linguistics: System Demonstrations*, pp. 55–60, 2014.

[20] M. Maru, F. Scozzafava, F. Martelli, and R. Navigli, "SyntagNet: challenging supervised word sense disambiguation with lexical-semantic combinations," *Proceedings of the 2019 Conference on Empirical Methods in Natural Language Processing and the 9th International Joint Conference on Natural Language Processing (EMNLP-IJCNLP)*, pp. 3532–3538, 2019.

A Multi-modal AI Approach For AGVs: A Case Study On Warehouse Automated Inventory

Ferran Gebellí Guinjoan[1], Erwin Rademakers, Abdellatif Bey Temsamani
Flanders Make
Lommel, Belgium
[1] email: ferran.gebelli@flandersmake.be
Gorjan Radevski[3], Tinne Tuytelaars
KU Leuven, ESAT
Leuven, Belgium
[3] email: gorjan.radevski@esat.kuleuven.be

Matthias Hutsebaut-Buysse[2], Kevin Mets, Tom De Schepper, Steven Latré, Erik Mannens
University Of Antwerp - imec
Antwerpen, Belgium
[2] email: matthias.hutsebaut-buysse@uantwerpen.be
Hugo Van hamme[4]
KU Leuven, ESAT
Leuven, Belgium
[4] email: hugo.vanhamme@esat.kuleuven.be

Abstract— **We present a multi-modal AI approach for Automated Guided Vehicles (AGVs) to perform autonomous warehouse inventory monitoring. A vision module detects and tracks the goods and registers them to the inventory when the confidence score is high. Moreover, we use uncertain detections to direct the AGV to better viewpoints that could lead to new inventory counts. Navigation is done with a Reinforcement Learning (RL) agent trained to perform directed exploration in previously unseen warehouse settings. Because there is not a pre-defined route, we implement a robust way to merge detected items to avoid double counts. We also use speech as an easy way to provide instructions to the AGV.**

Keywords- AI based autonomous systems; Automated Guided Vehicles, multimodal AI; navigation; deep learning; neural networks; reinforcement learning; warehouse monitoring & management system; automated logistics & inventory

I. INTRODUCTION

Inventory is done manually by humans in many logistic and industrial warehouses, which is a slow and costly procedure. Automated inventory analysis is potentially faster, safer and more accurate [1]. To perform automated inventory monitoring, two main tasks need to be achieved: count the goods and move autonomously through the warehouse.

Regarding the counting of goods, supervised AI vision techniques have proven good performance for detection of many types of objects [2]. However, accuracy depends on the amount and quality of training data, and often it is hard to reach very high accuracy values. For the inventory application, a requirement is to have as few labeled examples as possible. Otherwise, the implementation in a real setting would be infeasible if a lot of manual labeling is necessary each time a new product is introduced.

To move autonomously through the warehouse, many industry settings use Automated Guided Vehicles (AGVs). Classic navigation pipelines typically need to construct a map by scanning the environment with sensors, such as lidars [3], while manually driving the AGV. Sometimes the usage of floor markings or fiducial landmarks (e.g., reflectors) are used as well. These approaches do not only require an updated map, but also require a different module to set destinations or missions with waypoints, meaning that a high set-up time for new or modified environments is needed. Because of the increasing variability in warehouses, it is common that rack configurations are modified after short periods of time. This exposes the need for an increased flexibility in the whole navigation approach.

In this work, we show how multi-modal AI is leveraged to overcome current limitations and perform an inventory in a pure exploration manner without previously knowing the rack configuration. We demonstrate a proof of concept in a real-time AGV forklift (Figure 1), which exploits spatial-temporal data to increase accuracy and robustness.

Figure 1. AGV used for integration and experiments

Regarding the detection of goods, by using the video stream, lidar data and the forklift position we avoid the need to detect all objects in all frames, and detecting at least once each object becomes sufficient. Moreover, it is important to reject false positive counts to avoid adding wrong detections to the inventory. We deal with this problem by setting a high confidence threshold, which increases the object count only when the model is certain about the existence of the object. However, the information in low confidence detections is still valuable, and we use it to direct the navigation module to uncertain areas. This allows to actively interact with the environment and get better viewpoints. In many cases, this will lead to high confidence detections, and as a consequence to new counts in the inventory.

In terms of robustness, the challenge is to avoid counting twice the same object, so we add tracking between frames. Furthermore, as exploration can lead to revisiting some places after a while, we implement a robust merging strategy to avoid counting again objects seen in the far past. This is an issue that existing navigation solutions do not face because they navigate on a mission with manually selected waypoints on a map.

To explore an unseen environment, we use a Reinforcement Learning (RL) agent, which is trained through trial-and-error in simulation to explore a warehouse while being directed by an external module.

Operators need a fast and easy way to interact with AGVs. We introduce a module that allows operators to give instructions via speech commands. This way, the cooperation between humans and machines becomes smoother

In previous work [4], we focused on the multi-modality between speech and vision to detect objects given speech cues. The RL navigation modality was also present, but only available in simulation as a digital twin which was synchronized with the real-world vehicle. In this work, we have a higher focus on the vision modality and how it interacts with the RL navigation. Furthermore, we have implemented all the modules in a real platform, and we have switched from an autonomous off-highway vehicle into an AGV which performs warehouse inventory.

In Section II, the related work is reviewed. Section III specifies the multi-modal AI solution used to solve the automated warehouse inventory use case. Section IV describes the experimental platform and the results on the real setup. Finally, Section V gives conclusions and talks about future work.

II. Related Work

A. *Object detection and tracking*

There are two main approaches to perform Multi-Object Tracking (MOT), "tracking by detection" and "detection by tracking". "Tracking by detection" is a two-stage process: first an object detector [5] [6] [7] recognizes the objects of interest in a new frame, and then an object tracker uses the past detections to associate the new detections with the previous, creating tracks with consistent IDs across frames. CenterNet [8] is used in many trackers [9] [10] [11], as it is simple and efficient. The YOLO family of detectors [12] [13] are used in various trackers [14] [15] [16] due to the good trade-off between speed and accuracy. MOT tracking in 3D [17] [18] [19] follows the "tracking by detection" approach. One of the advantages of "tracking by detection" is that there are two modules, which can be easily combined, e.g., the same tracker can be fused with different detectors. In "detection by tracking", the tracking information is also used to improve the accuracy of the detector. In some cases [20] [21], a Kalman filter [22] is used to predict the tracks in the next frame. Transformer-based detectors can also be used in tracking [23] [24] to propagate boxes between frames.

Most methods keep only high confidence score detection boxes to perform data association, as detections with low confidences can be unrelated background objects. BYTETrack [16] implements a strategy with a second association round for low score detections, as an additional step, to filter potentially occluded objects. Generally, all methods use a similarity metric followed by a matching strategy for data association. SORT [25] uses location and motion cues to compute the Intersection over Union (IoU). Some methods [24] [26] [8] are robustified w.r.t. the camera movement by having motion specific parameters. Appearance similarity of Re-ID features is used in a standalone way in DeepSORT [27] and in a joint way with detections in other methods [15] [28].

Few works focus on re-tracking objects once they are lost and allow for re-tracking [29] only in a short future horizon.

B. *Navigation*

Currently, navigation with an AGV throughout a warehouse mostly relies on SLAM-based approaches in which the agent constructs a map, and simultaneously tries to localize itself within this map. Alternatively, beacons, floor markings or guiding rails might be placed in the environment in order to allow the AGV to navigate efficiently [30].

These approaches, however, have two main drawbacks. The first is that they are often not very flexible and require a lot of manual tuning and setup in order to operate. The second drawback is that navigation tasks are currently mostly limited to positioning the AGV to a specific point in space, through providing the coordinates of the location. Semantic tasks such as directly searching for a specific item, without knowing its location would require visiting the entire environment in a greedy fashion.

Reinforcement Learning (RL) is an alternative approach which is able to learn control policies in sequential decision-making processes through trial-and-error learning. In an RL setting, the agent executes actions in order to figure out the effect they have on the environment. An RL agent learns about the quality of its performed actions through feedback from a reward function.

RL has been applied successfully in navigation settings, e.g., in operating stratospheric balloons [31], or controlling robotic platforms [32]. However, RL is still facing an issue of sample efficiency. An RL-based approach generally requires a large amount of interactions with its environment in order to learn a successful policy. While there is a lot of research being conducted on making RL more sample efficient in navigation settings [33] it is still very impractical and unsafe to train an RL agent in the real-world [34] [35]. For this reason, RL is usually trained in simulation, where multiple environment instances can be parallelly run at a faster rate.

While training in simulation can generally alleviate the problem of sample inefficiency, a new issue arises due to the fact that the observations coming from a simulated sensor, and those coming from a real-world sensor are often very different. Real-world sensors are often noisier and are utilized in a larger variety of setups (such as weather conditions or lighting). A few different methods have been proposed before in order to solve this sim2real gap. Attempts have been made

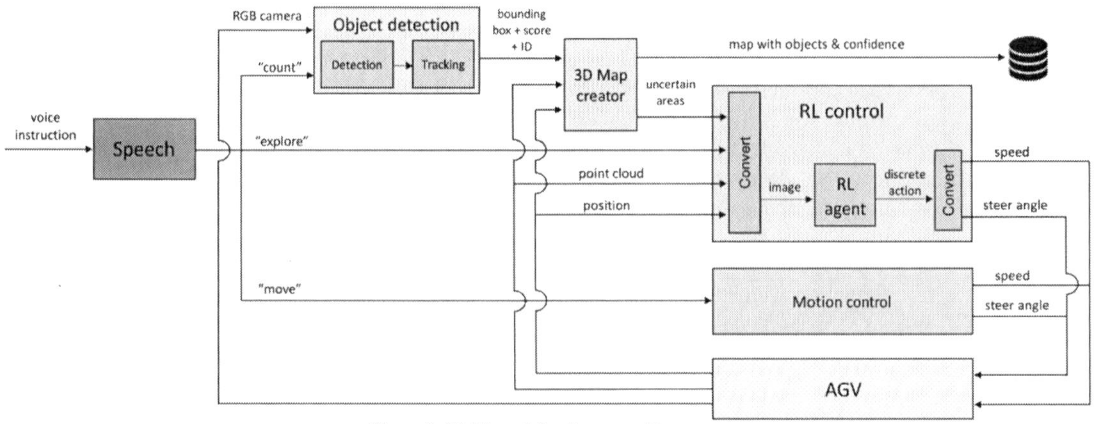

Figure 2. Multi-modal software architecture

at making the simulators more realistic [36]. This however resulted in the agent overfitting to aspects of the simulator [37] [38].

An additional benefit of RL based approaches over classic navigation approaches, is that they are able to solve semantically defined tasks. As classical navigation approaches are typically limited to navigation to coordinates. RL-based navigation approaches have outperformed such classic agents in specific settings in coordination-based navigation [39], and have been able to also handle tasks such as finding objects through only specifying the type of object, or exploring the environment in an intelligent and an efficient manner [40].

The usage of RL navigation to improve the confidence of detections in a map has also been addressed [41], but only in simulation.

III. Case study: AGV for Warehouse inventory

A. *Multi-Modal AI architecture*

Figure 2 an overview of the software architecture and interface between the platform and the different AI modules. Apart from the data that comes from the AGV (RGB image, point cloud and position) a voice instruction is the input that serves as user interface. The overall output are the control commands to the AGV and the map with the inventory counts.

B. *Spoken Language Understanding*

If the operator wants to give a speech command, he/she can either press a button and then start talking, or enable the open microphone feature and say a pre-defined keyword to indicate that an instruction will be given.

We have reused the user interface and AI model from a previous work [4] and retrained it to work in English for a new set of tasks. First, a command is available to start a new inventory session ("count" Figure 2). Then, there are 3 options available: steer the AGV manually, trigger the RL autonomous exploration ("explore" in Figure 2), or further give speech instructions to control the movement of the AGV ("move" in Figure 2), such as "forward", "a little bit to the left", or "stop".

C. *Reinforcement Learning Navigation*

We address the sim-2-real gap in the sensing part by using lidars, which are more robust to sensor noise. While lidar-based simulations are often very compute-intensive, our approach allows fast simulations by rendering obstacles into top-down images containing the lidar data, without any need for ray casting. Rack locations are similarly added as a second image channel, and a third channel contains past vehicle positions. This 3-channel image in the ego view (see Figure 3) determines the only input of the RL agent. The same 3-channel image is created in the real setup:

- The obstacles channel comes from a projection of the 3D lidar point cloud to the plane parallel to the floor.
- The second channel contains the areas to direct the exploration, which come from the detection module. A 3D point cloud is projected as in the first channel.
- The third channel contains the past trajectory, which is obtained by concatenating the last positions given by the AGV positioning system.

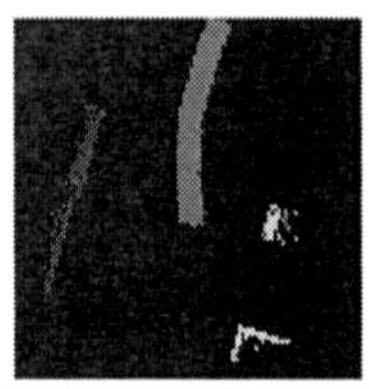
Figure 3. Input image to the RL agent. Blue are obstacles, green represents uncertain areas and red is the past trajectory

Simulations use a kinematic model of the AGV to bridge the sim-2-real gap in the acting part. The RL policy utilizes a discrete set of 15 actions, that map to specific steering angles and forward speeds. At a low speed (0.3 m/s) the vehicle can turn at 3 different angles (small, medium and large) to the left, and 3 to the right. The vehicle can also go straight. This makes a total of 7 actions, which are also available for backward moving. The 15th action allows to go forward straight at a higher speed (0.5 m/s). The simulation environments are randomly generated to create several rack configurations and generalize to any warehouse setting. We use Proximal Policy Optimization (PPO) [42] to train the agent.

D. *Object Detection and tracking*

The detector uses an RGB image as input and produces bounding boxes with associated confidence scores. We do not use depth sensors or lidar. The reason is that training models which use these sensors would require 3D annotations, generally not available in industrial datasets. An alternative is to label point clouds, which is prohibitive, and therefore we opt only for 2D object detection applied on RGB images.

We use the 3D lidar sensor, available in the navigation module, to obtain depth information which is pixel-by-pixel aligned with the RGB images. This approach provides better depth accuracy than depth cameras. The point cloud from the lidar is projected on the camera plane, with some inflation proportional to the depth value, leading to higher inflation for closer points. This provides a richer depth image, as illustrated in Figure 4. The projection of a point cloud into a camera plane only works well only if the two sensors are mounted close enough, which is the case for our platform.

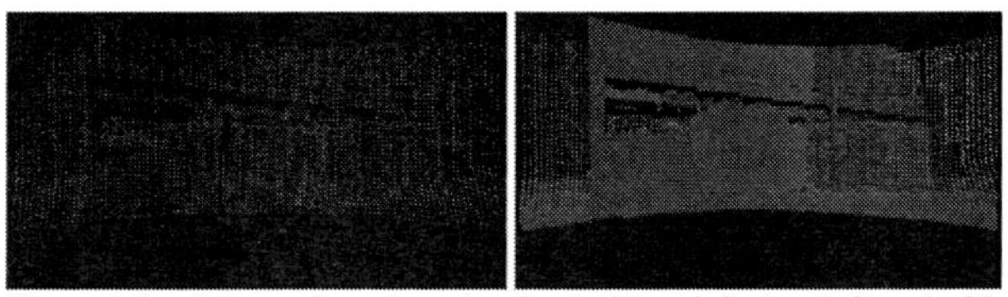

Figure 4. Depth image from the point cloud without inflation (left) and with inflation (right)

We choose the Yolov7 detector [12], as it is one of the latest open-source detectors with a better trade-off between accuracy and real time performance. Starting from a pre-trained version on COCO dataset [43], 4 videos recorded in the test warehouse have been annotated, making a total of around 1500 frames. The detector is trained to detect only one class, which is the cardboard box.

We select BYTETrack [16] as an object tracker, because it can be easily coupled with any other detector and yields to good accuracy in the MOT20 [44] benchmark. The main building block is a Kalman filter [22] with a constant speed model for the bounding box position and size of the detections. In most cases, trackers are employed in applications with a static camera and moving objects, while we use a moving camera with static objects. We have slightly modified the default version to be able to tune the covariance matrices Q and R of the Kalman filter in order to put a higher confidence on the detections (measurements) than in the model (constant speed motion). Especially when the camera is turning, the model will be less reliable, so we want to give higher importance to the new detections. Tracking provides unique IDs across frames, but does not solve the problem of tracking objects when they re-enter the camera FOV after some time. This will be addressed in the 3D map creator.

E. *3D map creator*

The individual 2D detections, the generated depth image and the AGV location in the warehouse are inputs to the 3D map creator, which is responsible to merge new detections to the ones in the map. This way, it keeps an updated version of the counted items locations, which are represented as cuboids with an ID, confidence score, internal point cloud, center, width, height and depth. The 3D map also keeps track of the uncertain areas, which are represented in the same way but with a negative value for the ID. Algorithm 1 shows the pseudo-code of the map creator, including also the object detector and tracker.

Algorithm 1: Pseudo-code of the inventory monitoring

```
Input: sequence S with image I, lidar point cloud L and vehicle
position P ; threshold for tracking T_t ; detection confidence threshold
for counting T_d ; position confidence threshold for counting T_p
Output: goods map M (list of objects with ID, confidence score,
point cloud and 3D cuboid)
Initialization: M <- 0
for I, L, P in S do
    Dets = detector(I)
    Tracks = tracker(Dets, T_t) % Tracks contain an ID, confidence
    score and bounding box
    Depth = project_pointcloud(L)
    for Track in Tracks do
        Depth_filtered = filter_depth(Depth, Track) % Depth with padding
        O_track = to_pointcloud_object(Depth_filtered, T_d) % object with
        point cloud, ID (<0 for uncertain) and confidence fields
        O_filtered = filter_poitcloud(O_track, T_p) % SOR, passthrough, SAC
        filters + ID becomes <0 if uncertain position
        O_world = to_world(O_filtered, P) % transform from ego view
        O_current = compute_cuboid(O_world) % add 3D box to object
        Test = overlap_test(O_current, M) % compare to all map objects
        if Test then
            M = merge_to_map(O_current, M) % discard new ID & merge
        else
            M = add_to_map(O_current, M) % new detection added to map
        end
        M = voxel_grid_filter(M)
        M = delete_uncertain_areas(M)
    end
end
Return M
```

Figure 5. Algorithm for inventory monitoring

For each new frame the algorithm iterates over the bounding boxes from the tracker. For each track, the corresponding depth pixel values are retrieved with a padding to discard pixels that may belong to the background. Then, depth values are converted back to a point cloud per detection. This point cloud goes through a filtering process that includes a Statistical Outlier Removal (SOR), a passthrough filter to remove far points and a SAmple Consensus (SAC) test: using the domain knowledge that boxes have flat surfaces and that they are never seen from above, we fit a plane and require it to be vertical in the world coordinate system.

At this point, we have for each detected object a point cloud, which generally contains points on the main surface of the box. There are two reasons to consider it uncertain:

- Uncertainty in the detector output: If the confidence score provided by the detector is below a certain threshold, then the corresponding object is marked as uncertain in detection.

- Uncertainty in the object location: In case the SAC plane is too far away, has a low number of inliers, or is not seen frontally (the boxes are too much at the side of the image), then the corresponding object is marked as uncertain in position.

The point cloud is finally transformed using the vehicle location into world coordinates, and a 3D cuboid that encloses the point cloud is computed.

Then, all the detections are merged with the map. There are two possibilities:

- The ID of the current detection is already in the map. In that case, the default option is to merge it with the map's object with the same ID. However, it could be the case that the 2D tracker fails, so an overlapping volume comparison is done with all the other detections already in the map, and if there is enough overlapping, the current detection is merged with the map object with more overlapping volume.
- The current detection is not in the map. The same overlapping test is done as in the case above. If there is not enough overlapping, it is a new detection, and a new object is initialized in the map. Otherwise, the new detection is merged into the matched object in the map.

When a detection is merged to one in the map, the point clouds are concatenated and then reduced using a voxel grid filter. The confidence is updated to the maximum of the ones being merged, and the centroid and vertex locations are updated fitting a cuboid to the point cloud. Since only one surface per box is considered, the cuboid corners are extended so each dimension is bigger than a user defined minimum object size. The current vehicle position and relative viewpoint respect the detection are used to know the direction of the extension.

Uncertain detections are merged in a similar way as certain ones. Certain and uncertain detections are never merged between them. When an uncertain detection with a particular ID becomes certain, all the uncertain data is deleted. Moreover, whenever there is a certain detection being added or merged to the map, nearby uncertain detections are deleted. Finally, in case that the AGV gets close enough to an uncertain detection and it remains uncertain, the object is completely discarded, since after having a good viewpoint the certainty did not increase enough, so it is assumed to be a detection false positive.

IV. EVALUATION

A. *AGV forklift platform*

An open experimental platform has been built on top of an AGV, automating a standard pallet forklift [45]. Localization is provided by a commercial system with reflector landmarks with known positions across the warehouse. Triangulation allows to get the AGV position with an accuracy of the order of few centimeters.

Two Ouster OS1 lidar with 64 vertical layers have been used. They have a vertical field of view of 45° and a maximum range of 120 m. They are placed in the front and the back of the AGV, and they are merged into a single point cloud that has a full 360-degree coverage. A camera (Zed mini) is used for inventory detection and is placed at the front of the forklift.

Figure 6 illustrates the hardware architecture and principal communications in the AGV. Robot Operating System (ROS) is used as a middleware to provide communication between the different perception modules. Then, control commands are sent to a motion module via ethernet, which is responsible for executing the actions on the AGV. There is a safety system mainly based on safety scanners that stops the forklift in case of an expected imminent collision.

The dynamics of the forklift can be summarized in the kinematic bicycle model [46]. This model is used in the RL training bridge the sim2real gap in the actuation. In Figure 7 the vehicle model can be seen.

The kinematics for a forklift AGV are defined by the following equations [47]:

$$\dot{x} = V(t)\, cos\, \theta(t)$$
$$\dot{y} = V(t)\, sin\, \theta(t)$$
$$\dot{\theta} = \frac{V(t)\, tan\, \delta(t)}{l - a\, tan\, \delta(t)}$$

The following values apply for this work AGV: l = 1.5m, a = 0:15m The forward velocity is denoted as V and δ is the steering angle in radians.

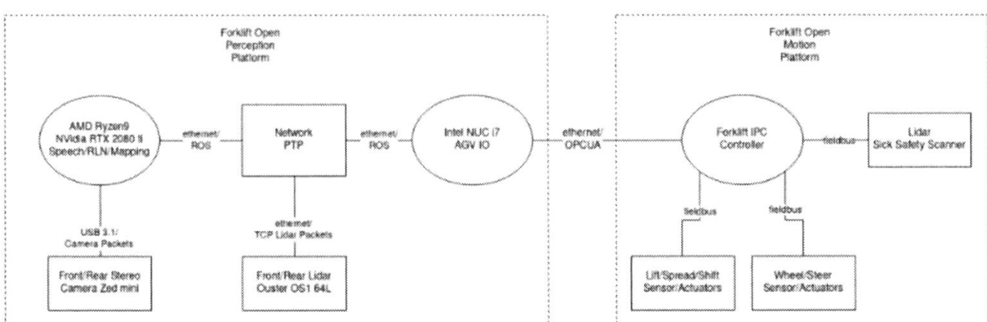

Figure 6. Hardware architecture

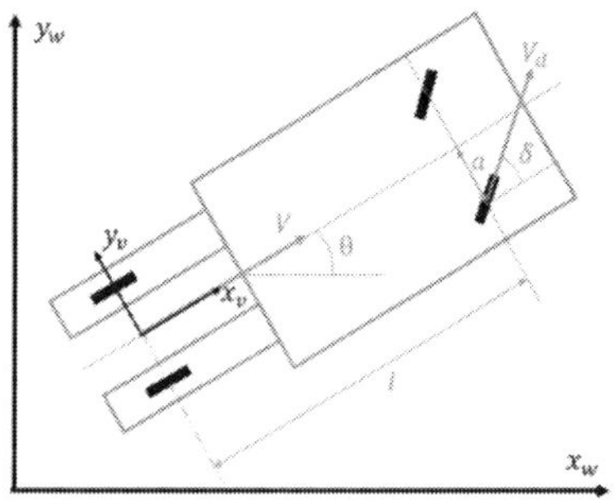

Figure 7. Bicycle kinematic model for AGV

B. *Experimental Results*

We have integrated all the algorithms in the forklift AGV platform and performed several online real-time experiments. Figure 8 shows the available inventory visualization in an experiment sequence. The locations of the racks are provided by the user and are only employed to improve the visualization, as they are not part of the algorithm. In the Figure 8 top image it is seen how several boxes in the middle rack have already been detected while in another rack there are uncertain detections. White points denote areas with low detection certainty, while grey points correspond to low certainty in location. Those areas direct the navigation to move closer, and once better viewpoints are obtained, they become certain detections that are added to the inventory, as seen in the middle image. Finally, in the bottom image it is seen how after performing a loop around the middle rack, the previous 2 racks are seen again, but only new objects are added to the inventory count. Detections that are assigned to an object already in the map are merged, and the object location is slightly adjusted accordingly if necessary.

TABLE 1 contains the results for object detection. We have used a test subset of 188 frames of around 30 seconds where the vehicle goes towards a rack and then performs a turn. The *"Detector alone"* row contains the results of the detector without any tracking or merging on the map. Then, the following rows represent the results for different ablations on the map creator, where the thresholds to track (T_t) and to count (T_d, T_p) are modified. *H* represents a version where the several thresholds for the position certainty are high, while *L* is for low values. We denote as $T_t=0$ the case where the 2D tracker is not used. The results include the precision and recall values, as well as the number of detected uncertain objects that are remaining in the map at the end of the sequence. A distinction is done between remaining uncertain objects that would become true and false positives if added to the count.

Although accuracy values in the *"Detector alone"* are high, all versions with the 3D map creator have a higher precision and similar or higher recall. Depending on the thresholds to track the objects and to count them in the inventory, the trade-off between precision and recall changes. In our application a high precision would be desired, while we expect to improve the recall by the active navigation. Results show there is still room for improvement in the directed exploration, since there are several true positive uncertain detections that were not yet included in the map. Alternatively, counting and position thresholds could be further reduced to count those uncertain detections and increase the recall, but that would reduce precision. Results show how the usage of a 2D tracker ($T_t \neq 0$) helps to avoid false positives, as seen in the TABLE 1 uncertain detections.

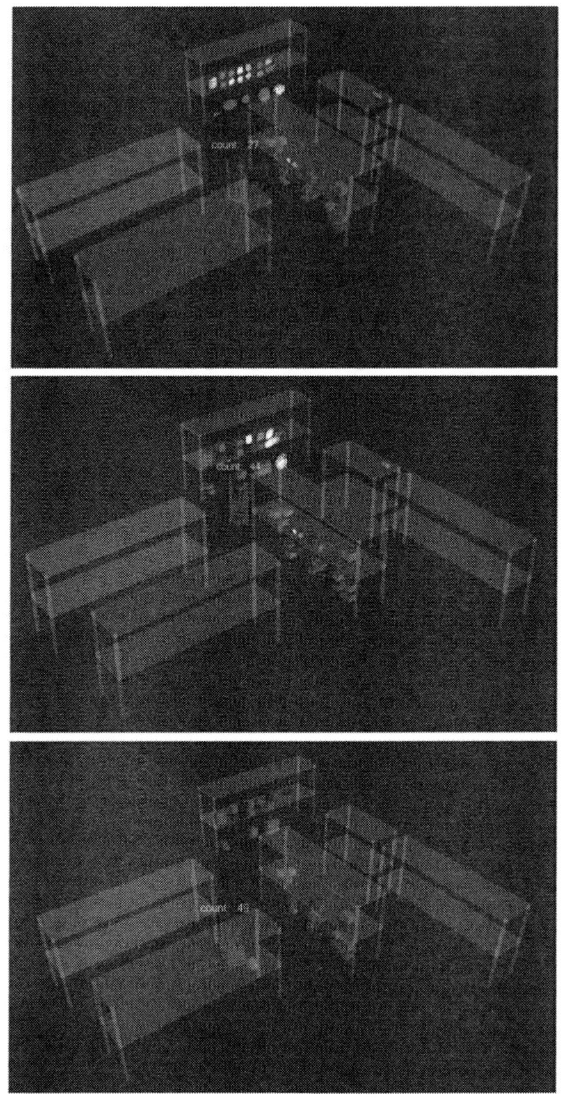
Figure 8. Sequence of the forklift around some racks in a warehouse.

TABLE 1. RESULTS OF THE OBJECT DETECTION

	Precision	Recall	Uncertain (T/F)
Detector alone	0.89	0.85	-
T_t=0.3, T_d=0.9, T_p=H	1	0.76	9/0
T_t=0.3, T_d=0.5, T_p=H	1	0.81	7/0
T_t=0, T_d=0.5, T_p=H	1	0.81	7/7
T_t=0.3, T_d=0.9, T_p=L	0.96	0.86	5/0
T_t=0.3, T_d=0.5, T_p=L	0.97	0.89	3/0
T_t=0, T_d=0.5, T_p=L	0.94	0.86	3/8

Results show how, by using spatial-temporal information of the same object while actively navigating to obtain better viewpoints, we can rely in a less accurate detector and achieve higher accuracy results on the high-level task of inventory count. This directly translates into a faster set up of the detector (less required labeled data, less time doing hyperparameter tuning, etc.), which is critical to reduce the implementation time of the solution in a new or modified warehouse. In this direction, the usage of an instance segmentation detector would have provided pixel level detections, which could be better matched to depth information leading to better position accuracy in the map. However, this would have increased the inference rate and the labeling effort. Our results show, how by post-processing the lidar data and registering to the inventory only detections with high position accuracy, a bounding box detector is enough instead of a more advanced pixel level instance segmentation detector.

V. CONCLUSIONS

The multi-modal approach presented in this work showed how uncertain detections in the vision module can be used in a navigation module, in our case based on RL, to improve the accuracy of the high-level task of warehouse inventory monitoring. If navigation can get better viewpoints directed by the detection module, the accuracy of the object detector is highly increased when applied to a time sequence. For a feasible industrial implementation, the set-up time in new environments should be minimal, and this work has proven how by considering uncertainty in the detections, a fast detector that is not accurate enough at frame level can achieve high accuracy at a task level.

The merging approach used to create the 3D map ensures that the same object is not counted twice. This is necessary in case of exploration which might re-visit the same areas. However, the current approach assumes that in each inventory session no objects are moved or removed. This is a limitation that needs to be addressed in future research.

This work also showed how the sim-2-real gap in RL can be addressed to successfully navigate in an unknown environment. Moreover, the navigation and the inventory modules are loosely coupled, which extends flexibility. The navigation module could be combined with other types of tasks where directed exploration is needed, such as finding an object or as intelligent patrolling. Beside the warehouse management application, the presented approach could also be used in other domains such as AGVs in agriculture or construction applications. We foresee future work on the RL navigation module with extended evaluation of the directed exploration navigation. We expect a performance comparison both in the simulation and real world setups between agents trained with different reward functions (e.g., general coverage vs directed exploration).

ACKNOWLEDGMENT

This research is done in the framework of Flanders AI Research Program (https://www.flandersairesearch.be/en) that is financed by EWI (Economie Wetenschap & Innovatie), and Flanders Make (https://www.flandersmake.be/en), the strategic research Centre for the Manufacturing Industry who owns the AGV infrastructure. The authors would like to thank everybody who contributed with any inputs to make this publication.

REFERENCES

[1] A. Gunasekaran, H. Marri, and F. Menci, "Improving the effectiveness of warehousing operations: a case study," *Industrial Management & Data Systems,* vol. 99, no. 8, pp. 328-339, 1999.

[2] J. Moon, S. Lim, H. Lee, S. Yu, and K.-B. Lee, "Counting System Based on Object Detection Using Deep Learning," *Remote Sensing,* vol. 14, no. MDPI, p. 3761, 2022.

[3] C. Stachniss, J. J. Leonard, and S. Thrun, "Simultaneous localization and mapping," *Springer Handbook of Robotic,* no. Springer, pp. 1153-1176, 2016.

[4] A. B. Temsamani et al., "A multimodal AI approach for intuitively instructable autonomous systems : a case study of an autonomous off-highway vehicle," *The Eighteenth International Conference on Autonomic and Autonomous Systems,* pp. 31-39, 2021.

[5] S. Ren, K. He, R. Girshick, and J. Sun, "Faster R-CNN: Towards Real-Time Object Detection with Region Proposal Networks," *Advances in neural information processing systems,* vol. 28, p. 1137–1149, 2015.

[6] K. He, X. Zhang, and J. Sun, "Deep Residual Learning for Image Recognition," *Proceedings of the IEEE conference on computer vision and pattern recognition,* pp. 770-778, 2016.

[7] P. Sun, Y. Jiang, et al., "What makes for end-to-end object detection?," *Proceedings of the 38th International Conference on Machine,* pp. 9934-9944, 2021.

[8] X. Zhou, D. Wang, and P. Krahenbuhl, "Objects as Points," in *arXiv preprint arXiv:1904.07850,* 2019.

[9] P. Tokmakov, J. Li, W. Burgard, and A. Gaidon, "Learning to track with object permanence," *Proceedings of the IEEE/CVF International Conference on Computer Vision,* pp. 10860-10869, 2021.

[10] Q. Wang, Y. Zheng, P. Pan, and Y. Xu, "Multiple object tracking with correlation learning," *Multiple object tracking with correlation learning,* pp. 3876-3886, 2021.

[11] Y. Wang, K. Kitani, and X. Weng, "Joint object detection and multi-object tracking with graph neural networks," *IEEE International Conference on Robotics and Automation (ICRA),* pp. 13708-13715, 2020.

[12] C.-Y. Wang, A. Bochkovskiy, and H.-Y. M. Liao, "YOLOv7: Trainable bag-of-freebies sets new state-of-the-art for real-time object detectors," in *arXiv preprint arXiv:2207.02696*, 2022.

[13] A. Bochkovskiy, C.-Y. Wang, and H.-Y. M. Liao, "Yolov4: Optimal speed and accuracy of object detection," in *arXiv preprint arXiv:2004.10934*, 2020.

[14] P. Chu, J. Wang, Q. You, H. Ling, and Z. Liu, "Transmot: Spatial-temporal graph transformer for multiple object tracking," *Proceedings of the IEEE/CVF Winter Conference on Applications of Computer Vision*, pp. 4870-4880, 2021.

[15] C. Liang, Z. Zhang, X. Zhou, and B. a. H. W. Li, "One more check: making “fake background” be tracked again," *Proceedings of the AAAI Conference on Artificial Intelligence*, pp. 1546-1554, 2021.

[16] Y. Zhang et al., "ByteTrack: Multi-object Tracking by Associating Every Detection Box," *European Conference on Computer Vision*, pp. 1-20, 2022.

[17] A. Patil, S. Malla, H. Gang, and Y.-T. Chen, "The h3d dataset for full-surround 3d multi-object detection and tracking in crowded urban scenes," *International Conference on Robotics and Automation (ICRA)*, pp. 9552-9557, 2019.

[18] X. Weng, J. Wang, D. Held, and K. Kitani, "3D Multi-Object Tracking: A Baseline and New Evaluation Metrics," in *International Conference on Intelligent Robots and Systems (IROS)*, 2020.

[19] H. Wu, W. Han, C. Wen, X. Li, and C. Wang, " 3d multi-object tracking in point clouds based on prediction confidence-guided data association," in *IEEE Transactions on Intelligent Transportation Systems*, 2021.

[20] P. Chu, and H. Ling, "Famnet: Joint learning of feature, affinity and multi-dimensional assignment for online multiple object tracking," *Proceedings of the IEEE/CVF International Conference on Computer Vision*, pp. 6172-6181, 2019.

[21] J. Zhu et al., "Online multi-object tracking with dual matching attention," *Proceedings of the European conference on computer vision (ECCV)*, pp. 366-382, 2018.

[22] R. E. Kalman, "A new approach to linear filtering and prediction problems," *J. Fluids Eng*, vol. 82, pp. 35-45, 1960.

[23] T. Meinhardt, A. Kirillov, L. Leal-Taixe, and C. Feichtenhofer, "Trackformer: Multi-object tracking with transformers," *Proceedings of the IEEE/CVF conference on computer vision and pattern recognition*, pp. 8844-8854, 2022.

[24] P. Sun et al., "Transtrack: Multiple-object tracking with transformer," in *arXiv preprint arXiv:2012.15460*, 2020.

[25] A. Bewley, Z. Ge, L. Ott, F. Ramos, and B. Upcroft, "Simple online and realtime tracking," *IEEE international conference on image processing (ICIP)*, pp. 3464-3468, 2016.

[26] J. Wu, J. Cao, L. Song, Y. Wang, M. Yang, and J. Yuan, "Track to detect and segment: An online multi-object tracker," *Proceedings of the IEEE/CVF conference on computer vision and pattern recognition*, pp. 12352-12361, 2021.

[27] N. Wojke, A. Bewley, and D. Paulus, "Simple online and realtime tracking with a deep association metric," *IEEE international conference on image processing (ICIP)*, pp. 3645-3649, 2017.

[28] J. Pang, L. Qiu, X. Li, H. Chen, Q. Li, T. Darrell, and F. Yu, "Quasi-dense similarity learning for multiple object tracking," *Proceedings of the IEEE/CVF conference on computer vision and pattern recognition*, pp. 164-173, 2021.

[29] T. Feng, L. Jiao, H. Zhu, and L. Sun, "A Novel Object Re-Track Framework for 3D Point Clouds," *Proceedings of the 28th ACM International Conference on Multimedia*, pp. 3118-3126, 2020.

[30] M. De Ryck, M. Versteyhe, and F. Debrouwere, "Automated guided vehicle systems, state-of-the-art control algorithms and techniques," *Journal of Manufacturing Systems*, vol. 54, no. Elsevier, pp. 152--173, 2020.

[31] M. G. Bellemare et al., "Autonomous navigation of stratospheric balloons using reinforcement learning," *Nature*, vol. 588, no. Nature Publishing Group, pp. 77-82, 2020.

[32] D. Shah, A. Sridhar, A. Bhorkar, N. Hirose, and S. Levine, "GNM: A General Navigation Model to Drive Any Robot," in *arXiv preprint arXiv:2210.03370*, 2022.

[33] E. Wijmans, I. Essa, and D. Batra, "How to Train PointGoal Navigation Agents on a (Sample and Compute) Budget," *21st International Conference on Autonomous Agents and Multiagent Systems*, pp. 1762-1764, 2022.

[34] H. Zhu et al., "The ingredients of real-world robotic reinforcement learning," in *arXiv preprint arXiv:2004.12570*, 2020.

[35] G. Dulac-Arnold et al. , "Challenges of real-world reinforcement learning: definitions, benchmarks and analysis," *Machine Learning*, vol. 110, no. Springer, pp. 2419-2468, 2021.

[36] M. Savva et al., "Habitat: A platform for embodied ai research," *Proceedings of the IEEE/CVF International Conference on Computer Vision,* pp. 9339-9347, 2019.

[37] A. Kadian et al., "Sim2real predictivity: Does evaluation in simulation predict real-world performance?," *IEEE Robotics and Automation Letters,* vol. 5, no. IEE, pp. 6670-6677, 2020.

[38] J. Truong et al., "Sim2Real: Lower Fidelity Simulation Leads to Higher Sim2Real Transfer in Navigation," in *arXiv preprint arXiv:2207.10821*, 2022.

[39] D. Mishkin, A. Dosovitskiy, and V. Koltun, "Benchmarking classic and learned navigation in complex 3d environments," in *arXiv preprint arXiv:1901.10915*, 2019.

[40] T. Chen, S. Gupta, and A. Gupta, "Learning Exploration Policies for Navigation," in *International Conference on Learning Representations*, 2018.

[41] D. S. Chaplot, M. Dalal, S. Gupta, J. Malik, and R. R. Salakhutdinov, "SEAL: Self-supervised embodied active learning using exploration and 3d consistency," *Advances in Neural Information Processing Systems,* vol. 34, pp. 13086-13098, 2021.

[42] J. Schulman, F. Wolski, P. Dhariwal, A. Radford, and O. Klimov, "Proximal Policy Optimization Algorithms," in *arXiv:1707.06347*, 2017.

[43] T.-Y. Lin et al., "Microsoft COCO: Commeon objects in Context," *13th European Conference in Computer Vision,* pp. 740-755, 2014.

[44] P. Dendorfer et al., "Mot20: A benchmark for multi object tracking in crowded scenes," in *arXiv preprint arXiv:2003.09003*, 2020.

[45] A. Bartic, "Autonomous vehicles can perform an increasing array of tasks all by themselves," Flanders Make, 28 April 2020. [Online]. Available: https://www.flandersmake.be/en/blog/autonomous-vehicles-can-perform-increasing-array-tasks-all-themselves. [Accessed 1 February 2023].

[46] P. Polack, F. Altche, B. d'Andrea-Novel, and A. de La Fortelle, "The kinematic bicycle model: A consistent model for planning feasible trajectories for autonomous vehicles?," *IEEE intelligent vehicles symposium (IV),* no. IEEE, pp. 812-818, 2017.

[47] K. Jung, J. Kim, J. Kim, E. Jung, and K. Sungshin, "Positioning accuracy improvement of laser navigation using UKF and FIS," *Robotics and Autonomous Systems,* vol. 62, pp. 1241-1247, 2014.

Moderate Loads Handling & Transportation by COBOTs and AMRs: Discussion of Different Architectures to Increase Payload & Reach and to Improve Operators Ergonomics

Abdellatif Bey Temsamani[1], Luka Ramaekers
Flanders Make
Lommel, Belgium
email[1]: abdellatif.bey-temsamani@flandersmake.be
Wilm Decré[2], Erwin Aertbelien, Frederico Ulloa Rios
KU Leuven
Leuven, Belgium
email[2]: wilm.decre@kuleuven.be

Raphael Furnemont[3]
Vrije Universiteit Brussel (VUB)
Brussels, Belgium
email[3]: raphael.furnemont@vub.be
Karel Vander Elst[4], Jonas Vantilt, Joris De Schutter
Flexible Robotic Solutions (FRS)
Leuven, Belgium
email[4]: karel.vanderelst@frsrobotics.com

Abstract — **Collaborative robots (cobot) open up many opportunities for industrial automation where interactions with Operators are required. These machines focus more on repetitive tasks, such as picking, to help workers focusing more on tasks that require problem-solving skills. Parts handling & manipulation, in production floor, logistics centers, etc. often require the combination of these two skills. In this paper, we present different architectures where cobots can cooperate with Operators to handle & manipulate moderate loads between 10kg-60kg and where the manipulation reach is further than 2 meters. Performing these loads repetitively only by Operators are the leading causes of injury and musculoskeletal disorders in production workplaces. The paper describes innovative methods for Operators-cobots interactions that require the minimal efforts for the Operator to successfully perform a load handling & manipulation task and leading to improved ergonomics in a workplace.**

Keywords - Cobots, Operator's ergonomics, load handling & manipulation, Gravity compensation, AMRs

I. INTRODUCTION

Collaborative robots, or cobots, can improve the working conditions of humans by decreasing the workload of human workers and by reducing the risk of workplace injuries such as Musculoskeletal Disorders (MSDs) [1]. Unlike the current traditional industrial robots, cobots are designed to provide more flexibility on the work floor and work safely alongside humans. In the human-robot collaboration paradigm, repetitive and precise tasks can be shifted to the robot while tasks that require more dexterity or problem solving ability can be assigned to the human [2]. An application where collaborative robots are useful, is the assembly task and more specifically the assembly of small batch size products with high variability. Currently available collaborative systems can be roughly categorized in two groups. The first group consists of light and compact cobots with a limited payload and reach, for example the UR3-5-10, KUKA LBR iiwa, ABB YuMi, Rethink Robotics Baxter/Sawyer, while the second group is formed by heavy and bulky devices with moderate payload and reach, like the Fanuc CR-35iA and Comau Aura. In between these two groups, there is a gap in the current commercial offers, for payloads ranging between 10 kg and 60 kg, and a large reach (> 2 meters) while retaining a compact solution. Market studies indeed confirm the largest growth potential for collaborative payloads to lie in the > 10kg payload range.

In a recent project [3], a research team represented by the authors of this paper, explored different innovative architectures to extend cobots payloads and spatial reach, while keeping a compact solution in an industrial floor. This paper summarizes these architectures, their implementations and achieved results.

The innovative contribution of this paper relies on extending a standard cobot' s payload and spatial reach by presenting different architectures to augment the cobots, both hardware and software wise, to make them compatible for moderate loads handling applications where operators stay strongly in the loop. A decision tree is also elaborated to facilitate the selection of one or a combination of architectures for a custom handling application with specific technical and safety requirements.

In Section II, studied architectures to increase cobots payload are described. In Section III, studied architectures to increase cobots spatial reach are summarized. Section IV discusses the experimental validation and achieved results. In Section V, a Decision Tree to facilitate the choice of one or combined architectures for moderate loads handling problems is presented and discussed. Conclusions are made in Section VI.

II. COBOTS ARCHITECTURES FOR INCREASED PAYLOADS

In this section, two architectures to increase cobot' s payloads beyond the specified payload of the cobot are discussed. Both architectures allow to augment the cobot with an extra system that shares the payload handling together with the cobot.

A. *Increased COBOT payload by gravity compensation*

In order to increase the payload of a cobot without changing its design, one solution consists of assisting the cobot with an additional structure that will handle most of the static torque due to the payload. A popular trend in robotics are gravity compensators which are either passive [4] or active [5]. These mechanisms can be placed directly on the joint and compensate for a payload (generally fixed if passive and variable if active). When placed on a joint directly, they have a torque-angle characteristic only function of the joint angle which is their main weakness as only few robot configurations (especially for robots with several degrees of freedom) have a static torque only dependent on one joint angle. More complex compensators can be used but they will generally require a change in the structure of the robot and are thus not discussed. Another option, close to what is already done for human Operators, is to combine a lifting platform with a cobot such as jib crane or a hoist. This interestingly creates a parallel structure (and not an open chain anymore) with a part of the system which can be fully actuated or under-actuated (jib crane) and another part actuated or even over-actuated (when 7 degrees of freedom are present in the cobot). Most of the work-space of the cobot is still available by using these platforms although this can cause a reduction of the number of degrees of freedom at the end-effector. A commercial solution based on this idea (CobotLift) already exists and increases the payload from 16kg (of a UR-16 cobot) to 30kg. The lifting system is a pneumatic one that has limitations in terms of kinematics. The first concept in our research proposes a passive lifting platforms using gravity compensators with improved kinematics [6]. A conceptual sketch of the combination of the proposed gravity compensation system and a cobot to increase the payload is show in Figure 1.

This compensation system acts as an advanced cantilever that compensates for the excessive weight above the cobot payload.

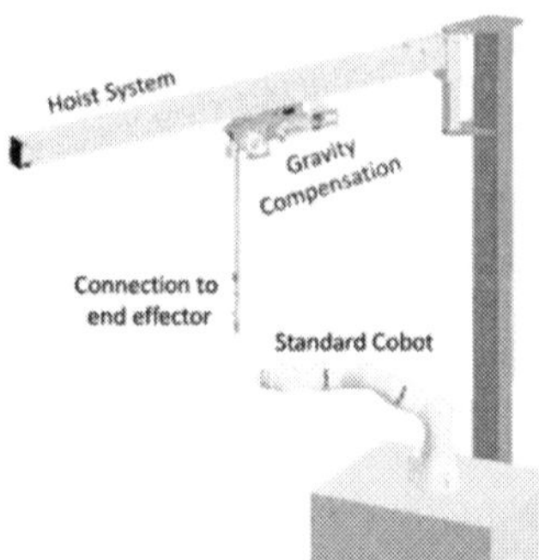

Figure 1. Sketch illustrating the proposed gravity compensation system to increase cobot payload

B. *Increased COBOT payload by industrial hoist*

The second concept of our research consists of combining the cobot with an industrial passive hoist system. The load is fully handled by the hoist while the cobot / robot acts as a guiding system. A conceptual sketch is illustrated in Figure 2. While the hoist compensates gravity, a robot with reduced payload guides a heavy load to a precise target position and orientation, for example during a transfer motion or an assembly process. A gantry supports the hoist, providing one or two degrees of freedom that are either passive or actuated. The robot could be replaced by a cobot. For extending its reach, the robot could be placed on a mobile platform (see Section III).

Different levels of integration between the motion controllers of the subsystems (gantry, hoist, robot, platform) are possible, resulting in different implementations for the overall task controller. A major concern is to protect the robot end effector against the occurrence of high forces due to modelling errors or disturbances (e.g., due to synchronization errors) in the overall motion control system. To this end, the robot end effector (red box in Figure 2) includes, besides a gripper, a 6D force/torque sensor and a 6D passive compliance.

III. Cobots Architectures for Extended Reach

In this section, two architectures to increase cobot' s reach are discussed. Both architectures are based on setting cobots in a wheeled unit that allows unlimited reach.

A. *Extended Cobot Reach by instructable AMR*

Autonomous Mobile Robots (AMRs) enable flexible and changeable small series production where 87% of the production time is going in transporting parts and components [7]. For parts transportation and handling in production floor, AMRs enable automation of these tasks, as they benefit of both, a flexible moving platform to automatically move, and a flexible manipulator, typically through a high degree of freedom cobot.

While in theory, the autonomous mobile system of the AMR would allow an unlimited reach of the manipulator system, synchronizing these two high-tech systems to deal with complex handling of various tasks, parts & environments, as well as having intuitive interactions with Operators remain a challenge in practice.

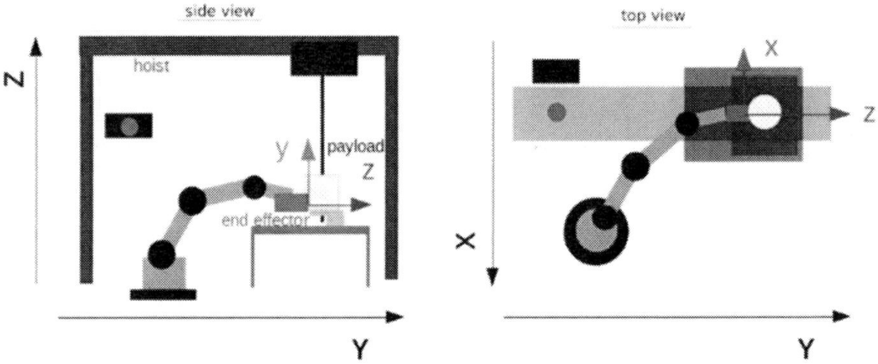

Figure 2. Schematic layout of robot-hoist co-manipulation

Our research platform consist of configuring a standard AMR by controlling individually or in synchro different parts of the AMR (i.e., manipulator / mobile platform) to physical support Operators, such that the AMR performs basic manipulation tasks (e.g., actively handling a part) while the Operators concentrate into precise actions (e.g., screwing parts to each other's). The first concept (Figure 3 - Left) consists of configuring an AMR to act as a 3rd hand supporting Operators to assemble parts (±10kg) in difficult poses. While the second concept (Figure 3 - Right) consists of configuring an AMR as a 'joystick' allowing Operators to organically interact with the full system in order to transport parts with moderate loads (±20kg) in an extended reach within a production environment.

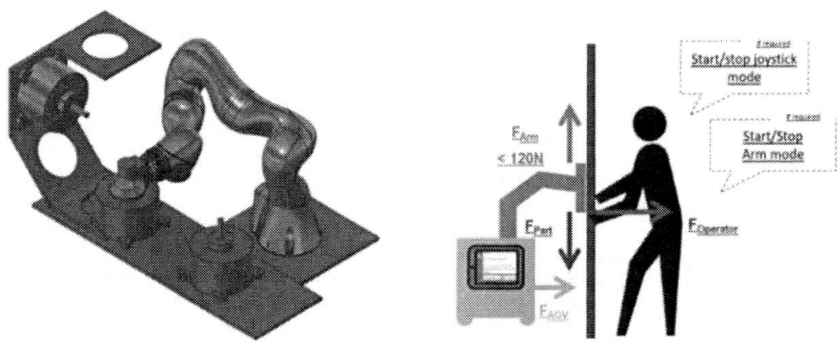

Figure 3. (Left) AMR configuration as a 3rd hand to support Operators, (Right) AMR configuration as a 'joystick' for part's transportation and handling with extended reach

The first case challenge consists of programing the manipulator to achieve difficult reach while smoothly collaborating with Operators, while the second case challenge deals with accurate control to synchronize between the manipulator & the mobile platform while interacting with Operators.

B. Extended Cobot Reach by Double Controlled AMR

Commercial AMRs (like the ones proposed in Section III.A) are provided with integrated mobile platform and manipulator and all safety around them. However, an AMR can also be achieved by combining a standard robot manipulator with a Wheeled Mobile Manipulator (WMM), designed from existing motorized wheels. On one hand, these WMM systems should be able to handle high payloads. On the other hand, they need to be able to move in a workspace only constrained by the environment. In case of shared control with a human Operator in order to carry heavy loads, this also requires that the platform can instantaneously move in all directions ("holonomic") and that the platform is able to quickly react to inputs of the human while jointly carrying a load. A typical solution is to use a highly powered, precise, holonomic platform, e.g., equipped with Mecanum wheels [8],[9]. These are however expensive, costly to maintain, and still limited with respect to the load they can carry. To avoid wheel slip, they also impose significant requirements on the floor on which the robot travels. Below, we present a control architecture that lessens the requirements imposed on the mobile platform such that a lower-dynamic platform with steered wheels can be used and wheel-slip can be tolerated, as long as an accurate pose estimate of the platform is available, even in cases where the platform needs to carry a heavy load. A control framework is proposed [10] that exploits the difference in the dynamics between the mobile platform and the robot manipulator in order to improve the accuracy and the bandwidth of the whole WMM. This framework uses two velocity-resolved constraint-based controllers using eTaSL [11], as shown in

Figure 4.

Both controllers use the same kinematic model of platform and manipulator and the same model of the human-robot interaction for jointly carrying load. The first controller ('platform eTaSL') however can only adapt the platform control input, i.e., desired velocity set-points for the mobile platform. It is not assumed that the mobile platform can execute these desired velocity set-points perfectly. It is however assumed that we can obtain a good estimate of the mobile platform pose and velocity via proprioceptive or exteroceptive sensors. The second controller ('arm eTaSL') determines the control input for all of the degrees of freedom of the manipulator, taking into account the measured mobile platform pose and velocity. The above results in a control architecture with two constrained-based controllers, one for the platform, one for the manipulator, where both controllers use the complete model of the robot system and task. For example, the platform eTaSL controller will also anticipate joint limits of the manipulator degrees of freedom by avoiding to move the platform in directions that will necessitate violating these limits. The manipulator controller will use its knowledge of the platform motion to compensate the errors of the platform eTaSL controller. Compared to a single constraint-based controller, this approach does not require additional modeling effort for the application developer since the same robot and task model is used for both controller.

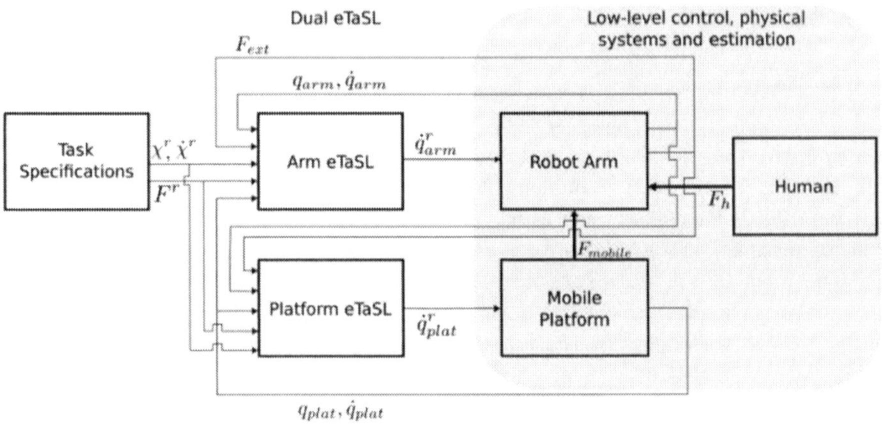

Figure 4. Control architecture for Wheeled Mobile Manipulator

IV. VALIDATION CASES AND ACHIEVED RESULTS

In this section, validation cases of all 4 architectures described in Section II & Section III are presented.

A. *Gravity Compensation increases Cobot payload by x2 for light loads (<8kg)*

The architecture presented in Section II.A, is implemented in Kuka Franka Emika Panda (payload 3kg). Using a jib crane, on which our gravity compensator is placed (Figure 5), the payload has been increased to 5,8kg. In this scenario, the gravity compensator can statically balance payloads between 0.8kg and 8.7kg over a stroke of 800mm which allows covering a large amount of the workspace of the cobot. Although the compensator can statically balance 8.7kg, due to internal friction, this is limited to 3kg dynamically as shown in Figure 6. This limitation is discussed in details in [6] and can be improved in future designs. By changing the level of compensation, the payload felt by the cobot can be kept minimal potentially allowing lower energy consumption for the cobot.

Scaling up the presented concept to deal with higher loads would require the redesign of the gravity compensators and use of more powerful motion components.

Figure 5. Jib crane with a gravity compensator (left – red dash line) coupled to a Franka Emika Panda Cobot (right). The payload of the cobot is initially 3kg (the gripper weighting already 0,8kg) and the manipulated load (black cylinder – green dash line) weighs 5kg

B. *Industrial hoist + robot increases payload by x2 for moderate loads (>15kg)*

The architecture discussed in Section II.B is implemented for heavy spools handling. As illustrated in Figure 2, the set-up includes a world reference frame *XYZ* and a robot end effector frame *xyz*. The robot is a 6 degrees-of-freedom (dof) KUKA KR16, with a payload of 16kg. The hoist is custom-made with one passive dof (along *Y*). The robot is equipped with an ATI/Schunk FTN-GAMMA force/torque sensor, a custom-made 6D passive compliance and a custom-made magnetic gripper which provided extra safety for the experiments (Figure 7). Both robot and hoist controllers are interfaced to a control pc on which the task controller is implemented in the *eTaSL* software framework for task specification and control of sensor-based robot tasks [11]. The interface to the robot reads its joint positions and sends desired joint velocities at 250 Hz with negligible delay. The interface to the hoist can only send on/off commands for up/down motions to the hoist controller. Hence, controlling the hoist from the pc is completely open loop. Moreover, the executed motion of the hoist is not completely deterministic, showing varying velocities and a considerable time delay which is also variable (~80ms). The poor-quality hoist interface and the high acceleration/deceleration of the hoist (up to 2.5 m/s^2) necessitated the use of the passive compliance in the gripper. We investigated three separate scenarios as reported below.

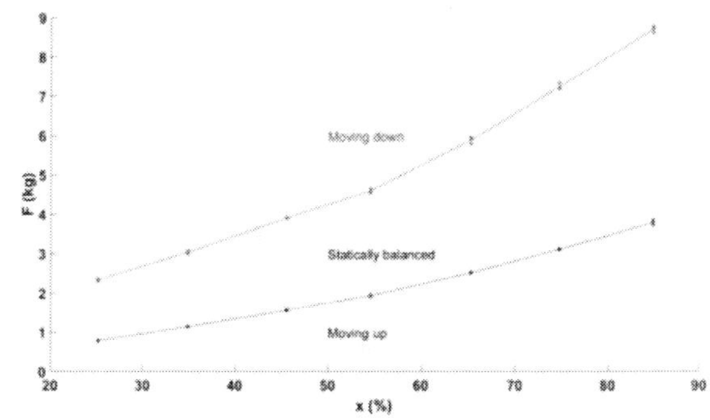

Figure 6. balanced weights versus gear ratio of the researched gravity compensation system

a) **Changing height of payload (Z)**
The main challenge for joint robot/hoist motion in the vertical direction was the synchronization between both motions. Our approach consisted of: 1) experimentally identifying the motion profile of the hoist and the variation of its time delay, and 2) controlling the end effector forces and torques to zero, while feeding forward the expected vertical hoist velocity profile to the robot. The measured vertical force for a payload of 11 kg and a change in height of 150 mm remains limited, both in executions where the open loop synchronization worked well (< 1N) or not (< 4N).

b) **Fast transfer motion along passive dof of hoist (Y)**
The main challenges were: 1) applying a suitably smooth motion profile for the payload to avoid oscillatory behavior (due to the dynamics of the passive hoist trolley subjected to a varying horizontal component of the cable force), and 2) avoiding large moments acting on the robot end effector. Accordingly, our approach consisted of: 1) applying a desired motion profile in translation that was continuous up to and including the derivative of

acceleration, and 2) adding a desired orientation profile of the end effector about its y (i.e., nearly vertical) axis to bring the main direction of the end effector (z) more in line with the acceleration/deceleration force (in the world's Y-direction.

Figure 7. (Left) Experimental set-up with annotated components, (Right) QR code of a video with the realizations

This was inspired by how humans would 'pull' the payload while limiting the moment applied to their arm. The orientation profile was made proportional to the desired payload acceleration. The scaling factor determines the amplitude of the rotation. In the experiments we started and ended the trajectory with the end effector oriented perpendicularly to the translation direction Y, and allowed a rotation amplitude of Θ=30° during the motion, which reduced the moment by a factor (1-cosΘ), hence by 13%. The traveled distance was 1.5 m in 10 seconds, resulting in a peak acceleration of 0.11 m/s^2. We used payloads up to 25kg, producing acceleration forces up to 28N for the payload only, but the moment on the end effector remained limited (< 2.1 Nm) thanks to this approach. No significant oscillatory behavior was observed.

c) **Force-controlled placement into a container**

This scenario assumes the payload has been transferred along Y and lowered to a 'sub-target' position that represents an appropriate approach position for the final placement (below gantry) in a 'target' position (not below gantry) that is subject to uncertainty (Figure 2). This final placement consists of two force-controlled motions (in X- and Y-directions, respectively) towards a wall of the container, followed by a brief activation of the hoist to deposit the payload while staying in contact with the two walls. This scenario did not pose any further challenge.

To summarize, even though this case considered a simple set-up (passive DOFs of the hoist, poor-quality interface of the hoist controller with the overall task controller), it was shown that a robot, in combination with a hoist, was able to manipulate a payload that exceeded its own capacity in industrially relevant scenarios.

C. *Instructable AMR allows an easy to operate mobile 3rd hand for Operators*

The architecture described in Section III.A., allows a modular configuration of a standard AMR to an organic mobile 3rd hand for Operators in assembly stations. The realizations of the two concepts described above are illustrated in Figure 8. Both realizations have been achieved by the following main steps, (i) programing the AMR in a compliance mode for a smooth collaboration with Operators (ii) modular configuration using pre-programmed modules for basic tasks (e.g., parts pick-up & drop-off) and programming new modules to make the process as intuitive as possible (e.g., automated gripping, active load estimation), (iii) easy interactions and instructions with / by Operators such as using interactive HMI (e.g., tablet) or hands-free control through natural speech interaction.

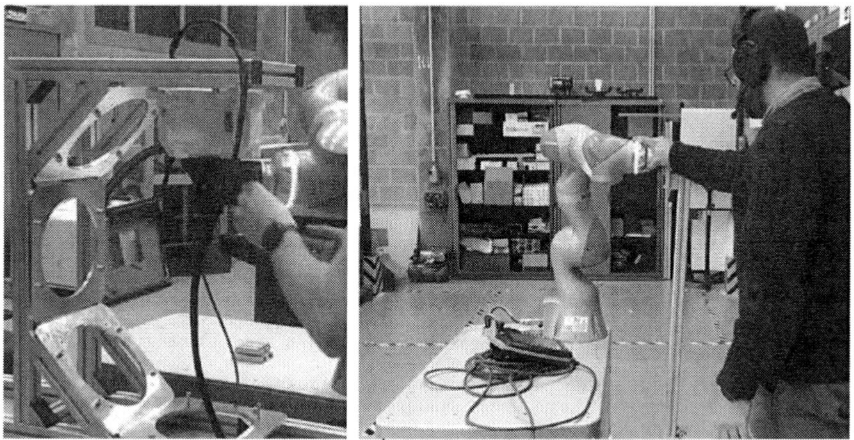

Figure 8. (Left) AMR in a 3rd hand configuration, (Middle) AMR in Joystick configuration, (Right) QR code of a video with the 2 realizations

D. *Independent wheels control for illimited reach for heavy payloads*

A mobile platform capable of carrying heavy payloads was designed using four wheel units. Two wheel units manufactured by KELO [12] were differentially actuated and two wheel units were passive caster wheels (cf. Figure 9-a). Each KELO unit has a payload of 125kg, which translates to a mobile platform evenly distributed payload of 500kg. Although this kinematic configuration is theoretically holonomic, significantly high wheel velocities can be necessary to move in directions perpendicular to the wheel axes of the drive units. These higher velocities can exceed actuator capability and can cause wheel slip, especially on uneven or dirty floors.

The architecture explained in section III.B can overcome the disadvantages of this kinematic design while at the same time being less expensive than e.g., Mecanum wheels and can handle uneven or dirty floors. To demonstrate this using an application where a load is shared between a wheeled mobile manipulator and a human Operator, a small Franka Panda 7-dof manipulator was mounted on top of this platform and two experimental cases were executed with good performance: one involving a pure positioning task and another involving a human-robot interaction on task.

Figure 9-b shows the results a motion of the platform where a significant disturbance occurs due to wheel reversal. It can be seen that the accuracy of the proposed dual controller architecture is significantly improved compared to a single constrained-based controller (85% in the motion direction and 57% in the other direction).

In a second case, an insertion under shared human-robot interaction has been performed (Figure 9-c) with significantly reduced interaction forces due to the imperfect motion of the mobile platform. Compared to a single constraint-based controller, the interaction forces in the vertical direction where dominated by the insertion forces and remained approximately the same, while there was a reduction of disturbance force of 50% in the motion direction and 25% in the direction perpendicular to the motion.

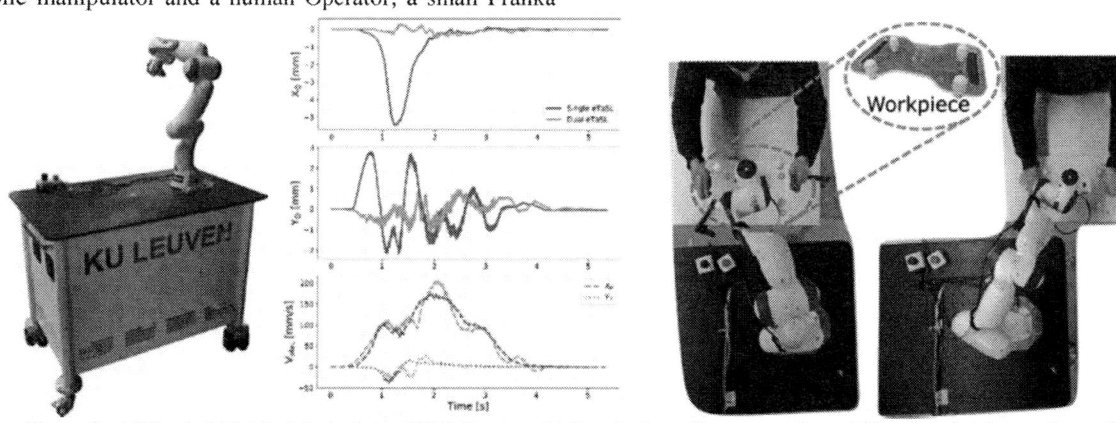

Figure 9. a) Wheeled Mobile Manipulator (WMM) set-up, b) Results for null space motion, c) Human robot interaction task.

V. Decision Tree for Cobot Based Handling Architecture

Depending on the handling application, a specific cobot-based architecture can be chosen. A decision tree to facilitate this choice is illustrated in Figure 10.

The decisions are made based on 3 main criteria: (i) the spatial distance where the load to be handled should travel versus the spatial reach of the cobot, (ii) the weight of the load to be handled versus the cobot maximum payload, (iii) the level of interactions with the Operators.

If the spatial traveling distance (reach) is below 2m (standard cobot reach), a standard cobot can be used if the weight of the part to be handled is lower than the cobot payload. Otherwise, gravity compensation architectures (section IIA / IIB) can be used to augment the cobot payload. Selection between architecture (IIA) or (IIB) can be made based on the number of degree of freedoms needed during the handling of the load versus the design budget / maturity of the solution. Architecture presented in Section IIA can offer high degree of freedoms but requires more design efforts and dimensioning of the system for moderate loads. While the architecture presented in Section IIB offers a high industrial maturity but with limited degrees of freedom to handle the parts.

If the spatial reach is higher than the standard cobots reach, a motion system will be needed to extend the reach. Standard AMRs can offer a direct solution if one looks for a plug & play solution without changing system's control and where enough budget is available (typically > 50k€).

If more flexibility is needed with regards the motion control of a cobot system, the architecture in Section IIIB presents a good decision. The mobile system can be configured and controlled in a custom way, with yet cost-effective components.

If more flexibility is needed for interacting with Operators, the architecture presented in Section IIIA presents innovative techniques to interact with a mobile cobot in terms of organic control and intuitive interaction.

Finally, the presented architectures can be combined to generate advanced custom handling systems driven by specific technical requirements, as well as by safety requirements with Operators in the loop.

VI. Conclusions

In this paper, we presented different architectures where cobots can cooperate with Operators to handle & manipulate moderate loads between 10kg-60kg and where the manipulation reach is further than 2 meters.

We explored different configurations that can be scaled-up for industrial usage starting from standard robots, cobots and mobile platforms. A summary of these configurations & how to select relevant one is given in the decision tree in Figure 10.

The paper describes different configurations illustrating how to make a standard Cobot and / or an AMR, flexible & smart handling systems that provide systematic and relevant assistance to Operators. Depending on the load to handle, the desired reach and the level of interactions with Operators, one single configuration or a combination of different configurations would be needed.

Future research will tackle limitations of current concepts and implementations to make them more suitable for large variety of loads & reaches, more modular in their control architectures to facilitate more interactions between multi-agents (cobot, mobile platform, Operator, etc.), as well as to make them more robust to deal with complex assembly parts, tasks and missions.

Acknowledgement

This research is supported by Flanders Make, the strategic research Centre for the Manufacturing Industry and the Flemish Innovation and Entrepreneurship Agency through the research project 'SMARTHANDLER_ICON' (project number: HBC.2018.0251). The authors would like to thank all project's partners for their inputs and support to make this publication.

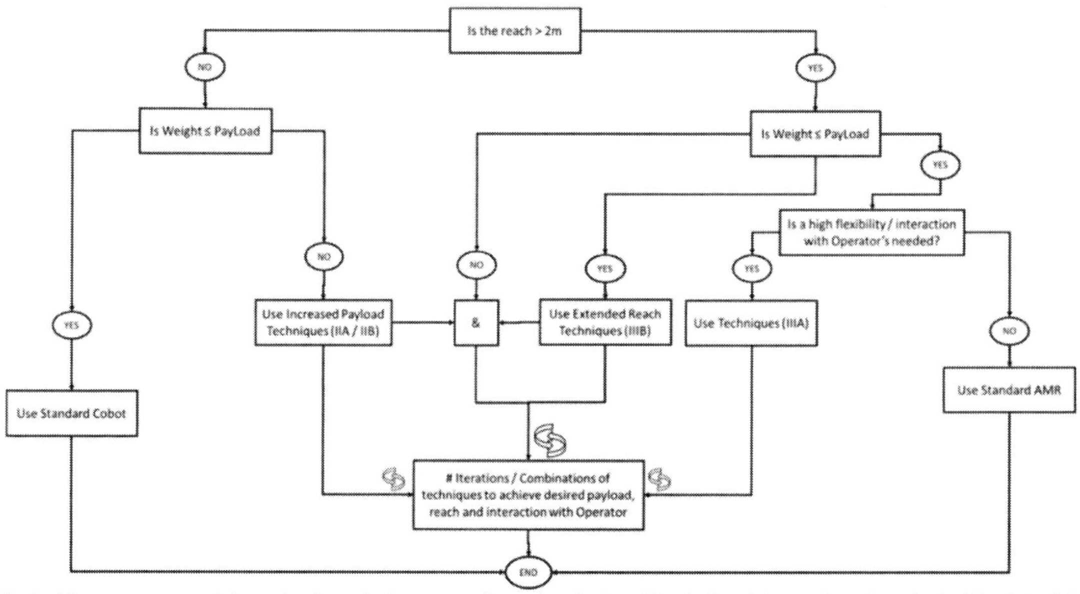

Figure 10. decision tree summarizing selection of relevant configuration for handling industrial parts based on desired load (weight), reach and interaction with Operator's

REFERENCES

[1] A. Own-Hill, Robots can help reduce 35% of work days lost to injury, blog.robotiq.com, May 26, 2016.

[2] Bauer, Andrea Maria et al. "Human-Robot Collaboration: a Survey." *Int. J. Humanoid Robotics* 5 (2008): 47-66.

[3] Flanders Make industrial research project: Smart Handing of Moderate Loads, SmartHandler ICON, VLAIO number: HBC.2018.0251, 2019-2022.

[4] Lee, Giuk, Donggun Lee, and Yonghwan Oh. "One-piece gravity compensation mechanism using cam mechanism and compression spring." *International Journal of Precision Engineering and Manufacturing-Green Technology* 5.3 (2018): 415-420.

[5] Kim, Jehyeok, et al. "Compact variable gravity compensation mechanism with a geometrically optimized lever for maximizing variable ratio of torque generation." *IEEE/ASME Transactions on Mechatronics* 25.4 (2020): 2019-2026.

[6] Furnémont, Raphaël, et al. "Prismatic gravity compensator for variable payloads." *IEEE Robotics and Automation Letters* 7.2 (2022): 3749-3756.

[7] Emmi Rajala, Autonomous Mobile Robots in small batch size production, Master of Science Thesis Faculty of Engineering and Natural Sciences Examiners: Professor Minna Lanz, Dr. Eeva Järvenpää October 2021

[8] B.E. Ilon, Wheel for a stable, self-propelled vehicle, German patent, 1974, DE2354404A, https://worldwide.espacenet.com/patent/search/family/023182799/publication/DE2354404A1?q=pn%3DDE2354404.

[9] B.E. Ilon, Wheels for a course stable self-propelling vehicle moveable in any desired direction on the ground or some other base. US Patent US3876255A, 1975, https://worldwide.espacenet.com/patent/search/family/023182799/publication/US3876255A?q=pn%3DUS3876255

[10] U. Caliskan, F. U. Rios, W. Decré and E. Aertbeliën, "Dual Constraint-Based Controllers for Wheeled Mobile Manipulators," 2022 IEEE 18th International Conference on Automation Science and Engineering (CASE), 2022, pp. 1001-1008, doi: 10.1109/CASE49997.2022.9926679.

[11] Aertbeliën, J. De Schutter, eTaSL/eTC: A constraint-based Task Specification Language and Robot Controller using Expression Graphs proceedings of the 2014 IEEE/RSJ International Conference on Intelligent Robots and Systems, Chicago, 2014.

[12] KELO Robotics GmbH. (Retrieved November 15th, 2022). [Online]. Available: https://www.kelo-robotics.com/technologies/#kelo-drives

Matlab/Simulink-Based Modeling for Industrial Electric Vehicle

Mouna Samaali
DRIVE EA1859
Univ. Bourgogne Franche-Comté
F58000, Nevers – France
Mouna.samaali@u-bourgogne.fr

Xavier Dessertenne
Métalliance Company
ZI La Saule,
F71230 Saint-Vallier – France
x.dessertenne@metalliance -tsi.com

El-Hassane Aglzim
DRIVE EA1859
Univ. Bourgogne Franche-Comté
F58000, Nevers – France
el-hassane.aglzim@u-bourgogne.fr

Patrick Dubreuille
Métalliance Company
ZI La Saule,
F71230 Saint-Vallier – France
p.dubreuille@metalliance-tsi.com

Abstract— **The land transport sector has passed through multiple phases of evolution in design, development, manufacturing of vehicles. In particular, the construction site continues to progress towards the autonomous vehicles (also called self-driving), which were one of its big trends and have become a hot topic in the industrial and academic world. By now, with this new technology of autonomous driving, we can ensure the safety by reducing the number of road accident, also the environmental impact and energy consumption is lessened. The modeling and simulation phases had become a mandatory step to design, characterize and simulate vehicle dynamics while reducing the cost of development. As they provide suitable test beds for the design and evaluation, the impetus of this study is to implement a model of a METALLIANCE's industrial Electric Vehicle based on Matlab/Simulink, that will be close to the reality. The model is implemented based on electrical equations associated with the power supply circuit. The model defines for real time the evaluation of various electric parameters in safe vehicle operation for these vehicles. This work will be completed by the design of a full simulator, which reproduces reliably the dynamic behavior of Métalliance construction vehicles.**

Keywords- Electric system modeling; Vehicle dynamics; Construction Machinery; Traction and Suspension control.

I. INTRODUCTION

The automotive and transportation industry are in perpetual evolution towards autonomous and electric vehicle (AEV), also known as automated car. It is seen as the important future technologies that will change the paradigm of mobility and facilities construction industry operations [1]. The Connected Autonomous Vehicle (CAV) is a system concept that can do driving maneuvers and tasks by itself, without human intervention, and communicate with its occupants and with external elements. The realization of this type of vehicle release humans from the driving task, reduce energy consumption, CO2 and pollutant emissions, and environmental impact. In addition, the autonomous car can improve safety by minimizing and preventing as possible the number of road accidents caused by the driver carelessness (most accidents are caused by human errors). But until now, replacing human driver with an autonomous driver is not guaranteed to avoid all problems. As the automated driving can impact positively the road traffic, it can also have a negative impact. Many works can be taken in order to minimize the negative externalities arising from automated driving [2].

The future of autonomous vehicle is in progress to be electric in order to have a complete vehicle which take the advantages of both autonomous vehicle and electric vehicle (EV) such as environmental benefits (C02 emissions and environmental pollution) and energy efficiency [3]. The combination of the EV and AV could facilitate automatically the charging when the Stage of charge is in short supply and prove the best scan and analysis of the environment by its artificial intelligence system to avoid any kind of collision with static or dynamic objects.

The wider application of AEV requires various real time vehicle operating tests under certain driving scenarios in order to determine if requirements are met for design. This process of development justifies the high cost and the long time taken to produce the final product. For that reason, modeling and simulation are becoming an important tool in solving this kind of problem and are considered as the best solution to dimension all components and achieve the best energy control strategy.

Vehicle modeling was invented to facilitate every kind of parameter change and analyze several powertrain configurations in a computer model before building the vehicle prototype. Thus, it can allow the final product to be well built and faster while reducing cost. Also, it is easy to engineers to examine the performance and energy aspects of vehicle powertrain configuration from a computer-based model than swapping motors in a real vehicle prototype.

This research is part of the Simulation of Autonomous Vehicle "SIMVA-2 "project funded by the French « France relaunch » plan. It is a bipartite link between the DRIVE laboratory and the METALLIANCE, company, which is intended to develop a simulator for an autonomous vehicle with an application to the confined industrial environment, in which the company's construction machinery operates. The objectives of this research project are to provide solutions for partial or total driving delegation of a construction vehicle in a controlled indoor environment, predict the physical behavior (electrical, thermal, etc.) of the various parts of the vehicle (engine, battery, perception/vision systems, etc.) and Train driver of this new mode of material transport.

Métalliance, a company specialized in the design of mobile machinery required for tunnel construction, designs, industrializes, manufactures, and markets mobile machinery used for the construction and renovation of tunnels. It has recently turned its attention to make its machines totally autonomous. Therefore, both modeling and simulation are obligatory required to design, characterize, and simulate the behavior of its mobile machinery on an industrial construction site, while reducing costs in the development phase. The aim of this study is to implement a METALLIANCE's electric vehicle model based on Matlab/Simulink that will be used to create a complete vehicle model. Create a vehicle model is then followed by simulation, an autonomous vehicle simulator will be built, which constitutes an easily accessible tool that represents artificially the real operation of Métalliance self-driving cars. This simulator allows reproducing in a more reliable way the dynamic behavior of these machines in their real environment with a huge number of scenarios, system configurations and driver characteristics.

This paper is divided into five parts. Section II outlines a brief introduction of electric vehicles and several electrical models existing in the literature. Section III presents the industrial environment of our case study: the characteristics of Métalliance mobile machinery and their ODDs (Operational Design Domain). Section IV constitutes a literature review of all steps followed to describe the dynamic behavior of a system in the form of a model. Whilst, the Section V introduces the vehicle system modeling based on Matlab/ Simulink, the validation on a real profile and the behavioral analysis. The present work ends with conclusion and Outlook.

II. LITERATURE ON ELECTRIC VEHICLE MODELS

A wide waste of energy and air pollution was resulted using construction machinery and influenced the health of humans and other human beings. Thus, to solve this problem, it is required increasing fuel efficiency and minimizing fuel consumption. The novel technology "Electric vehicle (EV)" allows both reducing air polluting and noisy mobility. The control of the torque and the speed through motor control was achieved by several electronics components such as transistor.

In the literature, several electrical construction vehicle models have been proposed to evaluate the vehicle energy consumption, examine the impact of different factors influencing the energy consumption and enhance the vehicle efficiency [4]. Most of these models was numerical models which are used most of the time in the first stages of the design process. The aim of these stages design of an energy efficient vehicle is to evaluate all parameters affecting the energy requirement based on a sensitivity analysis.

In [5], a Model-based optimization of an electric vehicle has been developed in Simulink environment. It was used to determine an optimization driving strategy aimed at reducing energy consumption while driving (prototype electric car that has been designed for the Shell Eco-marathon). In this case, genetic optimization algorithm was used. The model includes the vehicle, the electric motor, and the motor controller, the simulation was compared to the real measurements and the results has shown the similar optimized model to the real world. In this wise, a full efficiency of electro-mechanical power system is treated. Nevertheless, each change, like way of the route modeling or the driving conditions modeling, applied in on of electro-mechanical power subsystems must be experimentally evaluated. Also, the driver control system is considered in this model which has as inputs the reference vehicle speed or the accelerator activation.

In [6], a model optimization of the powertrain design has been developed. The system was applicated for the development of fuel cell electric vehicles which were vehicles with three wheels use a carbon-fiber monocoque pushed by a hydrogen fuel cell with a DC electric motor. In the model, the vehicle, and its subsystems (fuel cell, uphill climbing, electric motor, tires rolling resistances, aerodynamic drag, etc.) are simulated in AMESim and the dynamic behavior of the vehicle was analyzed. An optimization algorithm was employed to find the optimal driving strategy leading to least fuel consumption. The model was validated by the comparison of simulation results to results obtained on the track during the competition (Shell Eco Marathon competition).

In [7] The paper describes a numerical modeling of the vehicle powertrain; a vehicle takes part in the Shell Eco-marathon competition. The model includes the vehicle motion and the fuel consumption, it was validated using real measurements. An optimization strategy was employed leading to low fuel consumption.

A Multiphysics dynamical model of a fuel cell vehicle-based power train (urban-concept vehicle used for energetic races) has been developed in [8]. The modeling encompassed several vehicle behaviors such as the losses and consumptions of the power in each train devices, mechanical requirement, thermal behavior of fuel cell, etc... A global optimization algorithm has been integrated to the model in order to find out the best driving optimization according to the road constraints. The simulation results are compared and validated with experimental measurements (real results obtained at the Shell Eco-Marathon competition).

In the view of the METALLIANCE's machines complexity (two or three vehicle module), no previous modeling of industrial electric vehicles has been done before. Also, none previous established results in modeling defined the validation of all inputs/outputs is made of electrical modeling vehicle before.

III. MODEL DEVELOPMENT STEPS

Models are usually primarily defined in the scientific literature as a simplified representation of a real-world phenomenon. The model is highly close to the real-world vehicle system but it is simpler than the system it represents. The purpose of producing model is to enable the analyst to predict the dynamic behavior of any kind of system, to be a close approximation to the real world and incorporate most of its salient features. The steps involved in developing a model, used to design a powerful simulation are [9]:

- **Identify the problem**: Before proceeding with the modeling of a proposed vehicle system, it is necessary to define the inputs, the corresponding outputs, the temporal and spatial constraints, the traffic conditions, the stochastic elements, the study objectives, etc.
- **Formulate the problem:** Select the bounds of the system, the traffic conditions, the environment conditions, the control rules, and the security constraints. The purpose of this step is to define performance measures and quantitative criteria based on different system configurations. At this stage, formulate briefly hypotheses about system performance. Hence, Problems must be formulated as precisely as possible and specific outputs are defined for each problem.
- **Collect and process real system data:** Collect data on system specifications inputs variables. Generally, sensors are installed on the system and permanently record information about its environment, perception and data fusion algorithms are then used to extract useful information.
- **Formulate and develop a model**: Develop network diagram of the system based on the relationships that connect the different outputs to the different inputs.
- **Simulate and validate model:** Once the previous steps are checked and validated, all that remains is the simulation of the model from the real data and ensures that the model achieves the expected results. At this level, it is required to vary different input parameters over their acceptable range and checking the output in order to verify that the simulation model executes as intended by comparing its performance with the performance of the real system.

In the physical sciences, models are defined from mathematical tools (differential equations, recurrent equations, or partial differential equations), physical tools (generally used for vehicle systems) or computer tools (tools derived formalisms of AI (Artificial Intelligence)). In the case of our study, the electrical model was developed with extreme accuracy for every element based on different physical tools (mechanical block, thermal block, power electronic, electrochemical block, electric energy storage.

IV. INDUSTRIAL ENVIRONMENT AND OPERATIONAL DESIGN DOMAIN SYSTEM

In this paper, electrical modeling was applied to an industrial environment: vehicles developed by the company Métalliance. These latter designs two types of vehicles: the Multi Service Vehicles (MSV) or Train on Wheels vehicles, that meet specific specifications These vehicles are used to transport the concrete elements required for the construction of tunnel. The Train on Wheels vehicle has a leading vehicle and a trailing vehicle each with a driver cabin to facilitate the reversible operation without having to make a U-turn in small space. Both the leading and the trailing vehicles are of self-propelled type and can be used according to the required direction of travel at the same time. However, The Multi-Service Vehicle is a non-articulated vehicle with only one vehicle. Like the train on wheels vehicle the MSV is also designed to facilitate reversible operation. The vehicles currently used by METALLIANCE are available in three variants with respect to the power source used by the vehicles. The vehicles can operate on a diesel engine, a hybrid between diesel and an electrical engine or a completely electrical engine. They, primarily used to supply logistics to and from the Tunnel Boring Machine (TBM), so they have wheels, which allow them to traverse on flat grounds and even on concave surfaces inside the tunnels without the construction of rails inside the tunnel.

To date, METALLIANCE is developing Automated Guided Vehicles (AGV) to assist the driver in driving operation of the vehicle, facilitate logistics and storage operation in indoor and outdoor environment. The figure below depicts the MEATLLAINCE'S Multi Service Vehicle (MSV) design and its dimension.

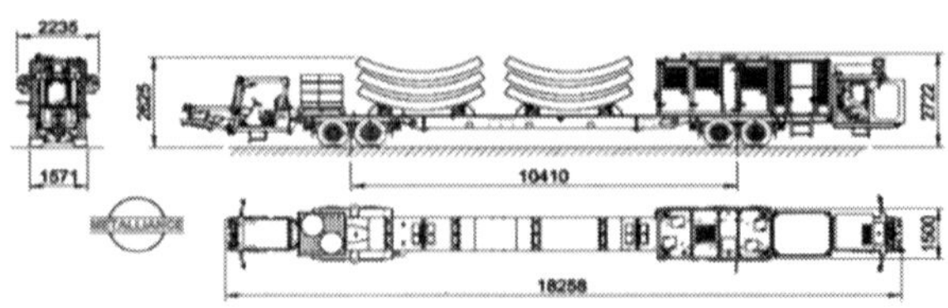

Figure 1. METALLIANCE's Vehicle (MSV).

V. SIMULATION, RESULTS, AND VALIDATION ON A REAL ROAD PROFILE (RENNES TUNNEL)

Electrical modeling vehicle allows to define the evaluation of all different electric parameters acting on the system at a time t in order to determine the electrical power needed for moving the vehicle forward. It constitutes the system of electrical equations associated with the power supply circuit. The electrical vehicle environment is modeled through the resistive torque applied to the electric motor. Therefore, the proposed electric model receives as input the drive cycle that the vehicle should execute (the given speed and road profile). This reference is given to a pilot model that gives as output a signal representative of torque request.

The followed figure (Figure2) depicts the overall diagram of the electric model vehicle based on the physical description of all forces acting on moving the vehicle [10]. This objective defines the first and second step of model development.

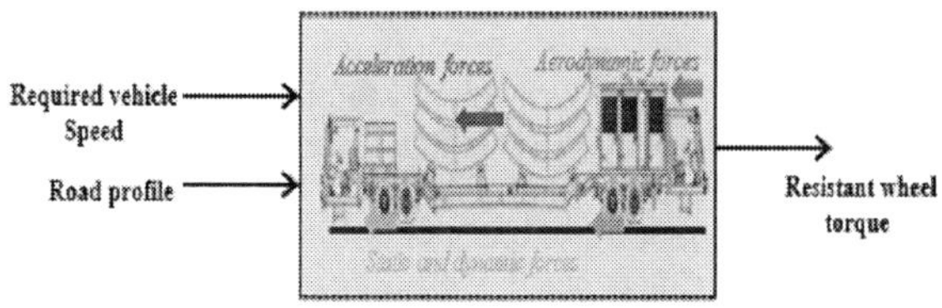

Figure 2- Electrical environment vehicle.

Based on the third model development step, specifications system (road profile and constraint speed vehicle) is recording from Rennes tunnel France and the value of these forces is leaning on the limit conditions that influence the vehicle.

To formulate the model and achieve the fourth model development step, the relationship that connect the different outputs to the different inputs is required. Thus, resistant wheel torque depends on the sum of these forces (rolling friction force, aerodynamic force, acceleration force, and the downhill-slope force) multiplied by the wheel radius. In fact, the rolling friction force is defined by the following equation.

$$F_r = C_r * m * g \quad (1)$$

Where C_r , m and **g** represent respectively the rolling resistance coefficient, vehicle mass (loaded and unloaded vehicle) and gravitational acceleration. The law states that the acceleration force is given by the multiplication of the acceleration a by the mass of the vehicle m.

$$F_{acc} = m * a \quad (2)$$

The force exerted by the air on the vehicle constitutes the aerodynamic force.

$$F_{aero} = 0.5 * S_{vehicle} * C_x * \rho * [V^2] \quad (3)$$

Where ρ represents the air density, $S_{vehicle}$ constitutes the section area of the vehicle, C_x is the aerodynamic coefficient and V is defined as the vehicle speed in m/s. Given that the maximum speed is 18 km/h, the vehicle is moving at low speed so we can neglect the aerodynamic force. Therefore, the resultant force down the slope (downhill-slope force) is given by this equation.

$$F_{slope} = m * g * sin(\alpha) \quad (4)$$

Where α is the slope angle. The sum of all these forces multiplied by the wheel radius results the resistant wheel torque, which is given by this equation

$$T_{wheel} = \sum Forces * R_r \quad (5)$$

By the value of the resistant wheel torque and the reduction wheel ration, the motor torque is defined.

$$T_{motor} = T_{wheel} * R_{ratio} \quad (6)$$

The motor speed is defined by from the vehicle speed.

$$S_{motor} = V * \frac{60}{2 * \pi * R_r} \quad (7)$$

And finally, the mechanical power is calculated by this followed equation.

$$P = S_{motor} * T_{motor} \quad (8)$$

All the vehicle parameters used for the simulation are defined in Table I.

TABLE I. REFERENCE VEHICLE DATA

Parameter	**Symbol**	**Value**
Maximum vehicle speed	V_{max}	*18 km/h*
Wheel radius	R_r	*599 mm*
Rolling resistance coefficient	C_r	*0,02*
Unlaoded vehicle mass	m	*15000 Kg*
Laoded vehicle mass	m	*40000 Kg*
Aerodynamic Coefficient	C_x	*1*
Air Density	ρ	*1.2 kg/m³*
Section area of the vehicle	$S_{vehicle}$	*6 m²*
Gravitational acceleration	g	*0.9419.81 m/s²*
Reduction Wheel ratio	R_{ratio}	*53*

Until now, the last step model development is still to validate. An overview of electric vehicle model implemented in Simulink is presented in Figure 3.

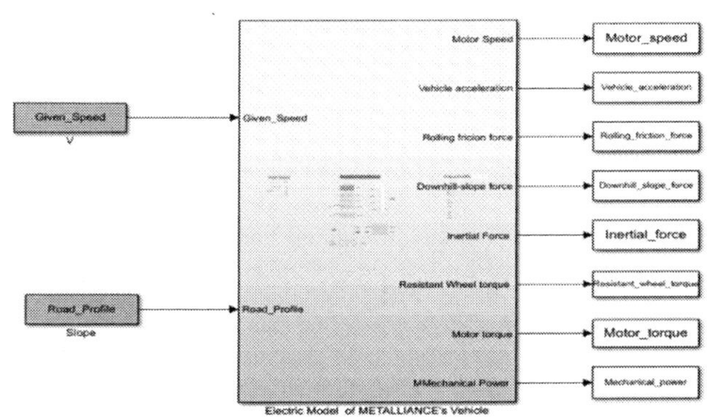

Figure 3- Simulink model of electric METALLINACE' s vehicle.

From a given speed and road profile, the system model estimates all forces applied to the machine, the resistant wheel and motor torque and passes through the relevant motor speed to evaluate the mechanical power needed to move the vehicle forward. The speed profile has a maximum speed of 18 kmph with two phases: the first where the vehicle is loaded and the second where the vehicle is empty. The modeling is applied to a Multi-Service Vehicle (VMS) vehicle.

In order to determine the level of fidelity model to the real world, the model should be compared to real data recorded for each real data of vehicle´s electrical system the driving operation vehicle. Indeed, an actual data has been recorded from driving task of the Métalliance Multi-Service Vehicle (VMS) in Rennes tunnel (France) (data of all electric parameters recording from vehicle operation inside Rennes tunnel during 238 minutes). Therefore, each real data of vehicle's electrical is compared to the corresponding in the simulation model in order to evaluate the performance and the accurate model development as is shown in Figures 4 and 5.

The model input (given speed) is divided into two phases: loaded (from 0 to 107 minutes) and unloaded vehicle (from 122 to 238 minutes). The first plot shows the comparison of the results simulation to their corresponding signals that were recorded during the measurement: vehicle's acceleration from the given speed input, the simulated rotational engine speed, the rolling friction force, and their corresponding signals that were recorded during the measurement. Moreover, the second plot shows the corresponding curves of the acceleration force, resistant wheel torque, motor torque and the mechanical power.

This simulation demonstrates approximately the overlapping curves of each parameter profile. As it shown by the simulation results, the diagrams resulting from the simulation and that of real data are substantially identical. This allows us to conclude that our model is faithfully close to the real world. Even, this work focus is made on the METALLIANCE's industrial vehicles, it could be used for other types of electrical vehicles. Just it must choose the road profile and speed and define the vehicle parameters.

VI. CONCLUSION

This paper presents the suitable process to implement an electrical model of a Métalliance Multi-Service Vehicle (VMS) in Matlab/Simulink environment, using the model development steps proposed throughout the literature. It falls within the framework of an autonomous vehicle, which can do driving maneuvers and tasks by itself. Therefore, methods and steps for modeling development have been exposed. The third model development step remains to study the operational design domain of the used system: environmental information, vehicle system characteristic and operation.

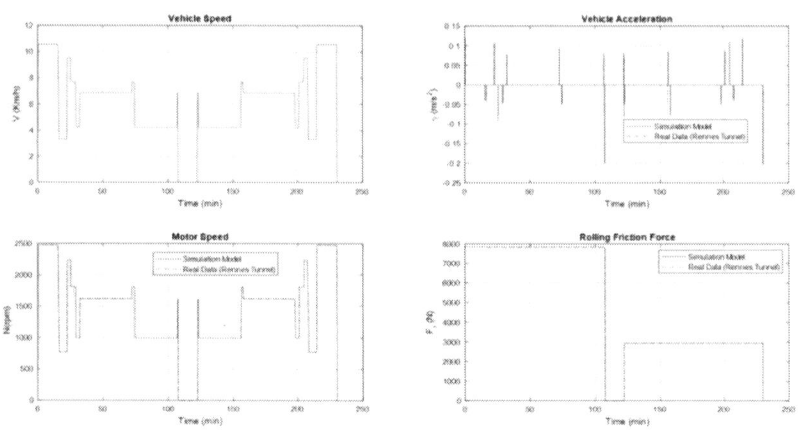

Figure 4-Vehicle speed, simulation results of electric model for vehicle acceleration, motor speed and rolling friction force.

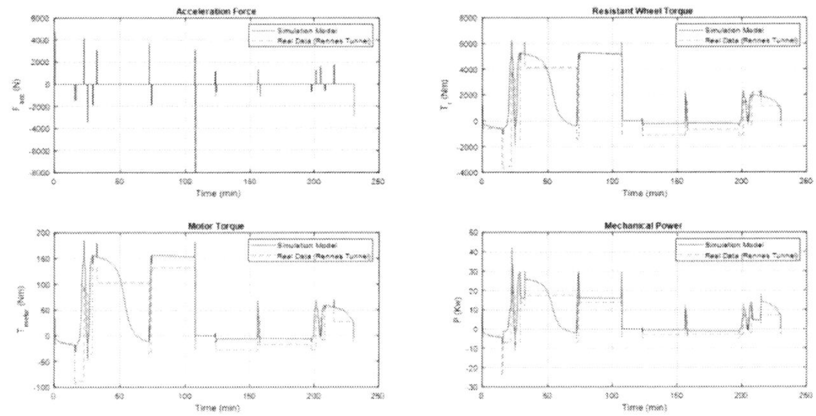

Figure 5-Simulation results of electric model for acceleration force, resistant wheel torque, motor torque and mechanical power.

Hence, an electric model vehicle has been developed based on the electrical equations associated with the power sup-ply circuit. It defines for real time the evaluation of various electric vehicle parameters. It has been validated by real world environment. We conducted its simulation by real data in order to validate its performance and achieve high accuracy in comparison with the actual world. The simulation result showed that the model is highly close to the real world. Some perspectives are considered in order to develop a simulator, which represents a virtual prototype of the real world that could be fast, efficient, and valuable.

The future work will focus on the development of the hydraulic and thermal vehicle model, then combining these models with the present work constitutes the step that achieves a complete Métalliance Multi-Service Vehicle (VMS) model. Thereby, the work will be completed by the design of a full simulator, which reproduces reliably the dynamic behavior of Métalliance construction vehicles.

ACKNOWLEDGMENTS

This research is part of the Simulation of Autonomous Vehicle "SIMVA-2 "project funded by the French « Plan de Relance », « France relaunch » plan-measures to preserve Research &Development jobs (. SIMVA-2 is a bipartite link between the DRIVE laboratory and the METALLIANCE, company, which is intended to develop a simulator for an autonomous vehicle with an application to the confined industrial environment, in which the company's construction machinery operates.

REFERENCES

[1]. Kichun, Jo.; Chansoo, K.; Myoungho, S. Simultaneous Localization and Map Change Update for the High-Definition Map-Based Autonomous Driving Car, Sensors 2018.

[2]. Serio, A.; Fausto, B.;Paolo, G.; Giovanna, M.; Rahul, P.;Marco, Po.;Luca,S. Impact of Driverless Vehicles on Urban Environment and Future Mobility. Elsevier, ETC 2019, Dublin, Ireland.

[3]. Chengxiang, Z.; ChunyanW. Integrated modeling of autonomous electric vehicle diffusion: From review to conceptual design, February 2021.

[4]. Stabile, P.; Ballo, F.; Mastinu, G.; Gobbi, M. An Ultra-Efficient Lightweight Electric Vehicle—Power Demand Analysis to Enable Lightweight Construction. Energies, 2021.

[5]. Targosz, M.; Skarka, W.; Przystałka, P. Model-based optimization of velocity strategy for lightweight electric racing cars. J. Adv. Transp, 2018.

[6]. Carello, M.; Bertipaglia, A.; Messana, A.; Airale, A.G.; Sisca, L. Modeling and optimization of the consumption of a three-wheeled vehicle. SAE Technical Papers, 2019.

[7]. Sawulski, J.; Ławryńczuk, M. Optimization of control strategy for a low fuel consumption vehicle engine, 2019.

[8]. Olivier, J.C.; Wasselynck, G.; Chevalier, S.; Auvity, B.; Josset, C.; Trichet, D.; Squadrito, G.; Bernard, N. Multiphysics modeling and optimization of the driving strategy of a light duty fuel cell vehicle. Int. J. Hydrog. Energy 2017.

[9]. Anu Maria; S. Andradottir, K. J. Healy, D. H. Withers, and B. L. Nelson. INTRODUCTION TO MODELING AND SIMULATION. In Proceedings of 1997 Winter Simulation Conference, State University of New York at Binghamton.

[10]. Wenge, Ch.; Hansch, K.; Arendarski, B.; Naumann, A. Electric vehicle simulation models for power system applications, Conference Paper 2012.

Utilizing Continuous Kernels for Processing Irregularly and Inconsistently Sampled Data With Position-Dependent Features

Birk Martin Magnussen
Opsolution GmbH
Ziegelstraße 17
34121 Kassel, Germany
e-mail: birk.magnussen@opsolution.de

Claudius Stern
FOM Hochschule für Oekonomie & Management
Hochschulzentrum Kassel
Garde-du-Corps-Straße 7
34117 Kassel, Germany
e-mail: Claudius.Stern@fom.de

Bernhard Sick
Intelligent Embedded Systems
Universität Kassel
Wilhelmshöher Allee 73
34121 Kassel, Germany
e-mail: bsick@uni-kassel.de

***Abstract*—Continuous Kernels have been a recent development in convolutional neural networks. Such kernels are used to process data sampled at different resolutions as well as irregularly and inconsistently sampled data. Convolutional neural networks have the property of translational invariance (e.g., features are detected regardless of their position in the measurement domain), which is unsuitable for certain types of data, where the position of detected features is relevant. However, the capabilities of continuous kernels to process irregularly sampled data are still desired. This article introduces a novel method utilizing continuous kernels for detecting global features at absolute positions in the data domain. Through a use case in processing multiple spatially resolved reflection spectroscopy data, which is sampled irregularly and inconsistently, we show that the proposed method is capable of processing such data natively without additional preprocessing as is needed using comparable methods. In addition, we show that the proposed method is able to achieve a higher prediction accuracy than a comparable network on a dataset with position-dependent features. Furthermore, a higher robustness to missing data compared to a benchmark network using data interpolation is observed, which allows the network to adapt to sensors with individual failed components without the need for retraining.**

***Index Terms*—machine learning; neural nets; continuous kernel; irregularly sampled data; reflection spectroscopy**

I. INTRODUCTION

Common machine learning methods assume that data is sampled consistently. That is, each instance of sampled data has the same shape and each data point always represents the same value. However, in real-world applications, data might often be sampled inconsistently due to factors like production inaccuracies of sensors measuring the data. In some cases, certain data points may be missing from a measurement as well. To facilitate this type of data, imputation of missing data points can be used to reconstruct the data [1]. Some methods also employ neural networks to reconstruct or correct data [2]. For certain types of network architectures, such as convolutional neural networks [3], continuous kernels have been utilized to circumvent these assumptions and to handle irregularly and inconsistently sampled data natively instead of needing special preprocessing [4] [5] [6]. Convolutional neural networks have the property of translational invariance, which is ill-suited to data expected to exhibit features at consistent absolute positions within the data sampling domain. Common examples of this type of data include spectral data, both optical and acoustic, where the relevant features may be intensity peaks at specific, consistent wavelengths rather than a wavelength-invariant feature of the intensity curve's shape.

To process data with position-dependent features natively when sampled irregularly and inconsistently, a novel method is proposed in this paper. It has been shown that neural networks, such as sinusoidal representation networks (SIRENs) [7] can be used as functions parametrized through their learnable parameters, making them suitable for use as continuous kernels. These kernels are shown to be capable of modeling global, long-term dependencies [4]. By utilizing such continuous kernels outside of the context of convolutional neural networks, our method is capable of natively processing irregularly and inconsistently sampled data with position-dependent features.

The rest of the article is organized as follows. Section 2 details the current state-of-the-art regarding continuous kernels. Section 3 discusses the definition of a continuous kernel. Section 4 introduces the new methodology utilizing continuous kernels. Section 5 shows the efficacy of the proposed method for processing spectroscopy data. Section 6 discusses potential future research into using continuous kernels for explainable AI. The conclusion closes the article.

II. RELATED WORK

Previous work on continuous kernels focuses primarily on applications in convolutional neural networks (CNNs) to handle irregularly sampled data. In [4], continuous kernels are utilized to process various types of sequential data, including irregularly sampled sequences. The article also performs an in-depth analysis of different types of continuous kernel parametrizations. [5] uses continuous kernels for convolutional neural networks to process non-grid bound data, such as representations of atoms in chemistry. In [6], continuous kernels are used to perform three-dimensional convolution on point clouds. However, as these articles all discuss the usage of continuous kernels for convolution in typical CNN architectures which all feature certain degrees of translational invariance, the methods discussed are not well suited for use with data containing position-dependent features.

Utilizing neural networks to represent a continuous function parametrized through the learnable parameters of the network, called implicit neural representation, has been previously analyzed by [8] [9] to model signed distance functions which are required for shape representation of 3D geometry. In [7], a network architecture called SIREN is proposed as an implicit neural representation for generic data, including audio, images, and signed distance functions.

III. Definition of Continuous Kernels

At its core, a continuous kernel is a function that assigns a weight to a data point at any given position [5]. Unlike in previous applications in CNNs, however, the position supplied to the kernel in our methods is an absolute position in the domain rather than a relative position to a convolution point.

To be able to represent continuous variants of typical weight kernels, the kernel function needs to be parametrizable with learnable parameters in such a way that the kernel function can ideally approximate any arbitrary function. It has been shown, that multi-layer perceptrons using sine nonlinearities, such as SIREN networks [7] can be used for such purposes.

Formalities

Small letters denote scalars, and small bold letters denote vectors. Capital letter variants of the former denote a set of the respective type. Subscripts on values indicate an index of the value within a containing set, superscripts indicate an index to the element of a vector.

Definition

Let $\mathbf{p}_i \in P \subset \mathbb{R}^n$ be the position of the value $d_i \in D \subset \mathbb{R}$ of the i-th data point of the set of data points D in an n-dimensional domain. A continuous kernel in the proposed architecture is now defined as a function

$$\psi : \mathbb{R}^n \mapsto \mathbb{R} \tag{1}$$

assigning a weight value to any position $\mathbf{p}_i$ in the domain. As shown in [4], such functions can be modeled and parameterized using implicit neural representations, such as Multi-Layer Perceptrons (MLP) using sine nonlinearities like SIREN [7]. In the proposed method, such an MLP serves as the function ψ. The MLP has n input neurons to input the absolute position $\mathbf{p}_i \in \mathbb{R}$ of a data point in the domain and one output neuron representing the assigned weight for the data point. The remaining model parameters of the kernel are the number and size of hidden layers in the MLP which can be adjusted to the problem to be learned. The MLP serving as the weight function ψ of a continuous kernel is not trained separately, but rather as part of the final network that the continuous kernel is used in.

IV. Application of Continuous Kernels in MLPs

Figure 1 shows the general structure of the proposed architecture. I shows the set of input data points to the model, each representing a value at a specific position within the measurement domain. In the proposed method, the first layer of the architecture, called the continuous feature layer, contains multiple independent continuous kernels (see II in Figure 1). For each of the independent kernels, the input consisting of an arbitrary number of data points is weighed using the kernel. Additionally, the input data might be sampled unevenly. To compensate for an uneven distribution of samples the local density of the sampled data points in the measurement domain is calculated (omitted in Figure 1). In the proposed method, kernel density estimation where the kernel size is a learnable parameter was used, but other methods for point density estimation can be used as well. Each data point is weighted by the inverse local density of data points at its position as proposed in [6]. The data points weighted by both the kernel and the inverse point density are shown in III in Figure 1 and are formally expressed in Equation 2. For each kernel, the weighted data points are reduced to a single value as defined in Equations 3 and 4 and as shown in IV of Figure 1. In the proposed method, a sum is used as the reduction operation, but other reductions, such as calculating the mean of the values are also considerable. Combining the reduced value of each

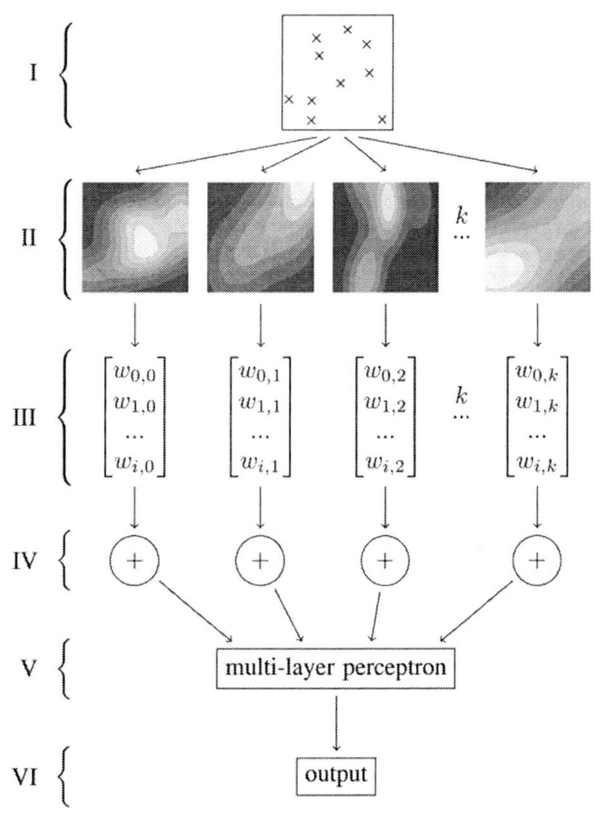

Fig. 1. Overview of a continuous feature network.

kernel into a vector results in an output feature vector of a fixed size depending on the number of independent kernels in the continuous feature layer. Since the continuous feature layer has reduced the input of arbitrary size to a latent vector of a fixed and predetermined size, the continuous feature layer can be followed with a typical neural network architecture, such as a multi-layer feed-forward network (see V in Figure 1). The output of this MLP then serves as the output of the entire network as depicted in VI of Figure 1. We call the proposed combination of a continuous feature layer followed by a multi-layer feed-forward network a continuous feature network. The continuous feature layer as described has three main model parameters: The number of kernels and the two parameters defining the shape of the kernels, being the number and the size of its hidden layers.

Formal Definition

Let the set Ψ be the set of multiple, independent continuous kernels ψ_k used in the continuous feature layer. In this set, each ψ_k represents one feature possibly present in the sampled data. Let $d_i \in D$ be the i-th data point in the input data with the position $\mathbf{p}_i \in P$ in the measurement domain. Let $\rho(\mathbf{p}_i)$ denote the local density of sampled data at position $\mathbf{p}_i$ in the domain. Then we define the weighted data points for each kernel as follows:

$$w_{i,k} := d_i \cdot \psi_k(\mathbf{p}_i) \cdot \frac{1}{\rho(\mathbf{p}_i)} \tag{2}$$

The components of the resulting fixed-size latent feature vector $\mathbf{v}$ are defined as follows:

$$\mathbf{v}^k(D, P) := \sum_i (w_{i,k}) \tag{3}$$

$$= \sum_i \left(d_i \cdot \psi_k(\mathbf{p}_i) \cdot \frac{1}{\rho(\mathbf{p}_i)} \right) \tag{4}$$

As the fixed size feature vector $\mathbf{v}$ is a function of the data points and their position, the feature vector can be expressed as a function of the following type:

$$\mathbf{v} : \mathbb{R}^i, \mathbb{R}^{i \times n} \mapsto \mathbb{R}^k \tag{5}$$

$\mathbf{v}$ describes the feature vector with a fixed size k as a reduction of an input of arbitrary size i for the data and $i \times n$ for the data's position for any i. Since the size of the feature vector $\mathbf{v}$ is fixed and does not depend on the input size i, the feature vector can be used as the input to a classical neural network architecture, such as a multi-layer feed-forward network, for an arbitrary input size i without the need to retrain the network.

V. EXPERIMENTS

The method is tested with a dataset from a sensor based on multiple spatially resolved reflection spectroscopy (MSRRS, [10]). The data was measured in vivo, alongside a reference measurement of the carotenoid concentration in the skin on a scale ranging from 0 to 12. The measuring system, similar to the one described in [10], consists of several light emitters of different wavelengths, as well as several light detectors. The datasets for training and testing are entirely distinct, having measured a different group of test subjects using a different set of MSRRS-based sensors.

The measured spectroscopic data is well suited for the use of continuous kernels and continuous feature networks as proposed in section IV. This is because the MSRRS-based optical data is yielded in the shape of a relative brightness given for certain discrete wavelengths and certain discrete distances between light-emitter-detector pairs. These discrete wavelengths and distances are neither sampled at regular intervals nor always at the same exact wavelengths. Due to production inaccuracies for the sensors, slight differences in the wavelength of the emitters exist. However, the peak wavelengths are known for each sensor's emitters, and can thus be accurately supplied as the position data for the continuous feature layer. In addition, in this kind of spectral data, it is expected that the relevant data is encoded not in the shape of features to be detected, but in the position of the features (here the absorption wavelengths of the carotenoids), making the proposed method suitable.

To evaluate the method, a continuous feature network with a continuous feature layer containing 64 continuous kernels is used. Each kernel is made up of a SIREN network, containing three hidden layers of 48 nodes with sine nonlinearities each. The continuous feature layer is followed by a hidden feed-forward layer with 64 nodes, followed by an output layer with one output for the predicted carotenoid concentration. This network has approximately 320k parameters.

For a comparison network, we use a multi-layer feed-forward neural network using a similar amount of parameters. This feed-forward network is supplied each emitter-detector pair as one node in the input layer, followed by a hidden layer of 256 nodes, followed by another hidden layer of 128 nodes, followed by an output layer with one output for the predicted carotenoid concentration, for a total of approximately 375k parameters.

A convolution-based model was also investigated but it has proved unable to produce meaningful predictions of the carotenoid concentration in human skin and is thus omitted

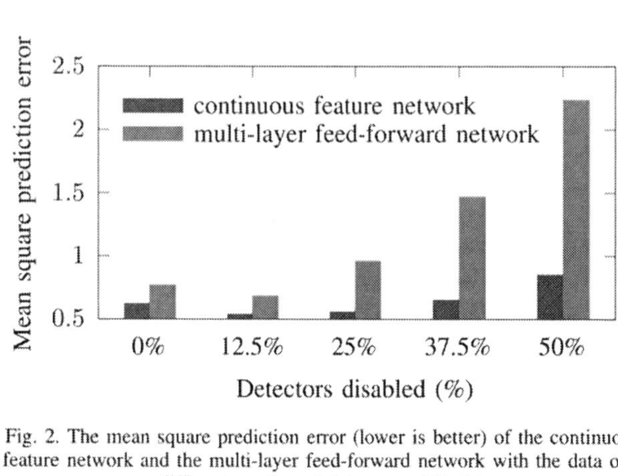

Fig. 2. The mean square prediction error (lower is better) of the continuous feature network and the multi-layer feed-forward network with the data of a different number of detectors withheld.

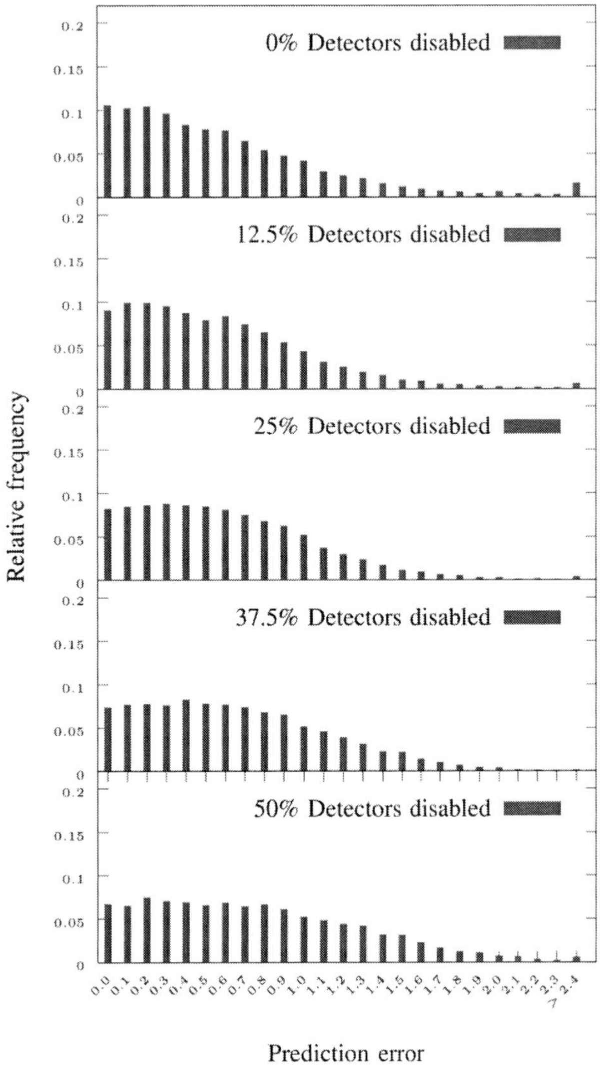

Fig. 3. A histogram of the prediction error of the continuous feature network at different numbers of light detectors whose data was withheld.

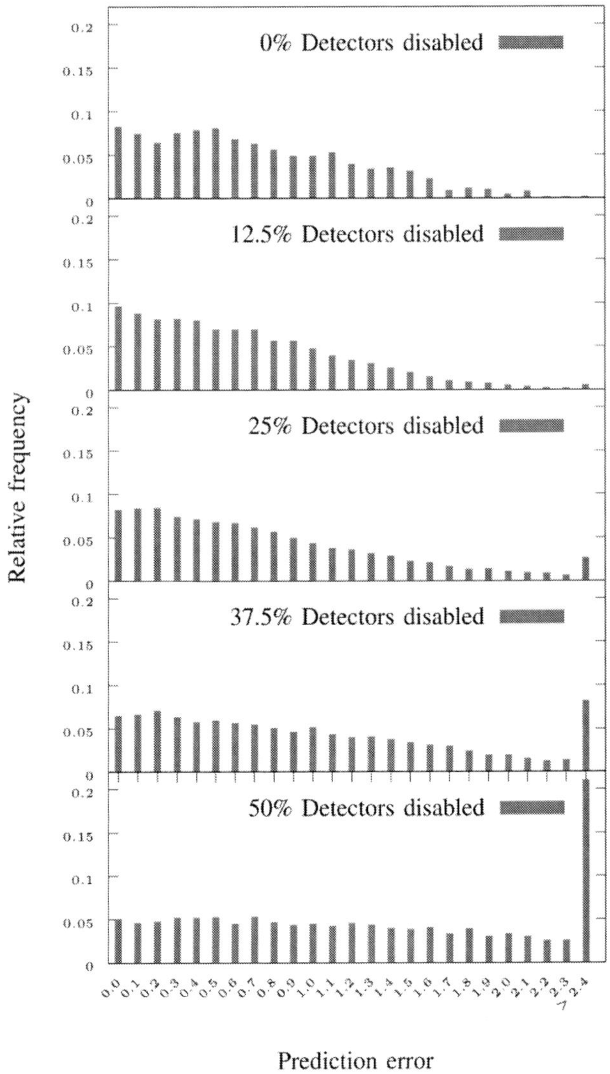

Fig. 4. A histogram of the prediction error of the multi-layer feed-forward network at different numbers of light detectors whose data was withheld.

from further analysis in this article.

Both networks were trained using the ADAM optimizer [11] and implemented using the LibTorch framework.

Figure 2 shows the accuracy of the proposed method compared to the accuracy of the comparison network. To show the ability of the continuous feature network to handle inconsistently sampled data, the prediction accuracy of the network was measured with the data of certain detectors withheld during inference. For each sample of data in the test set the detectors whose data was withheld were randomly picked, according to the number of detectors disabled. For the continuous feature layer, the missing data points were simply removed from the input vector. Due to the nature of the continuous feature network, it is capable of processing the shorter input vector without the need to retrain the model. For the multi-layer feed-forward network, the data was interpolated from the data of other detectors with a similar wavelength and emitter-detector distance. This is needed as the multi-layer feed-forward network is incapable of handling the shorter input vector without retraining. If no other data was available with a similar wavelength and distance, the value was set to 0 for the multi-layer feed-forward network. The results show that the continuous feature network outperforms the similarly-sized multi-layer feed-forward network for all investigated numbers of detectors whose data was withheld. The continuous feature network is able to achieve a mean square error of 19% lower compared to the multi-layer feed-forward network for the full set of input data. The improved prediction accuracy can be explained both by the high suitability of continuous feature networks for MSRRS data allowing an improved abstraction of the relationship between optical data and the reference carotenoid concentration in human skin, as well as because the continuous feature network is able to incorporate the actual measured wavelengths of the light emitters for each sensor as the position of the input data points. In addition, we see that the continuous feature network is able to give a stable prediction with more data missing compared to the multi-layer feed-forward network. This can also be seen in Figures 3 and 4. Figure 3 shows a histogram of the prediction error of the continuous feature network. In the different graphs, a different number of random light detectors were picked whose data was withheld from the continuous feature network. As the graph shows, while the amount of highly accurate precision lowers with more data being withheld, the amount of predictions with a large error (> 2.4) is not increasing significantly. This shows that the continuous feature network is capable of adapting to a lower amount of data being available to base its predictions on without the need for retraining. Figure 4 shows a histogram of the prediction error of the multi-layer feed-forward network. Similarly, the different graphs show the prediction error at different amounts of detectors whose data was withheld. In addition to a reduction in highly accurate predictions with more data withheld, the multi-layer feed-forward network quickly encounters an increase in predictions with a large error (> 2.4) once the amount of withheld data from disabled detectors increases to or above 25%. The slight increase of predictions with a large error occurring for the continuous feature network when no data is withheld is presumed to be due to an inaccurate input data point density estimation and will be subject to further investigation.

VI. Potential for Explainable AI

A side effect of the continuous feature layer is the resulting potential for explainable AI. As continuous kernels represent weights for each position in the measurement domain, we can deduct levels of importance of certain regions within the measurement domain from the encoded weights. The average of the absolute value of the weights over all kernels might be used as a measure of the importance of the data at certain points in the measurement domain. This may allow the use of the learned continuous kernels as an interpretable model [12]. However, as the magnitude of the input data at different positions in the measurement domain is not guaranteed to the normalized, any inferred importance from the kernel can be biased which will need to be accounted for. Similarly, the MLP being fed the latent feature vector will need to be considered when comparing the importance of the different kernels. Nonetheless, the usage of continuous feature layers as a tool for explainable AI is an interesting topic for further research.

VII. Conclusion and Future Work

This paper proposes the continuous feature network, a novel method to process irregularly and inconsistently sampled data with position-dependent features, such as optical or acoustic spectra. In addition, the continuous feature network is shown to outperform a comparable multi-layer feed-forward network with a 19% lower mean square error on predicting carotenoid concentration in human skin from optical multiple spatially resolved reflection spectroscopy data. This shows that the continuous feature network performed better at abstracting the relationship between the optical MSRRS data and the reference carotenoid concentration. Furthermore, this paper shows that the continuous feature network is capable of making stable predictions of carotenoid concentration in human skin with up to 50% of the data from the optical detectors withheld, while a comparable multi-layer feed-forward network exhibits a significant increase in predictions with a large error from 25% of the data withheld. Other potential use cases include similar types of data where samples may be irregular and features are position-dependent in the measurement domain, including other types of spectra, such as audio. Continuous feature networks also show potential for use as explainable AI and are worth studying further in this regard.

References

[1] A. R. T. Donders, G. J. van der Heijden, T. Stijnen, and K. G. Moons, "Review: A gentle introduction to imputation of missing values," *Journal of Clinical Epidemiology*, vol. 59, no. 10, pp. 1087–1091, 2006.

[2] P. K. Sharpe and R. J. Solly, "Dealing with missing values in neural network-based diagnostic systems," *Neural Computing & Applications*, vol. 3, no. 2, pp. 73–77, Jun 1995.

[3] Y. Lecun, L. Bottou, Y. Bengio, and P. Haffner, "Gradient-based learning applied to document recognition," *Proceedings of the IEEE*, vol. 86, no. 11, pp. 2278–2324, 1998.

[4] D. W. Romero, A. Kuzina, E. J. Bekkers, J. M. Tomczak, and M. Hoogendoorn, "Ckconv: Continuous kernel convolution for sequential data," *CoRR*, vol. abs/2102.02611, 2021.

[5] K. T. Schütt, P.-J. Kindermans, H. E. Sauceda, S. Chmiela, A. Tkatchenko, and K.-R. Müller, "Schnet: A continuous-filter convolutional neural network for modeling quantum interactions," in *Proceedings of the 31st International Conference on Neural Information Processing Systems*, 2017, p. 992–1002.

[6] W. Wu, Z. Qi, and L. Fuxin, "Pointconv: Deep convolutional networks on 3d point clouds," in *2019 IEEE/CVF Conference on Computer Vision and Pattern Recognition (CVPR)*, 2019, pp. 9613–9622.

[7] V. Sitzmann, J. N. P. Martel, A. W. Bergman, D. B. Lindell, and G. Wetzstein, "Implicit neural representations with periodic activation functions," in *Proceedings of the 34th International Conference on Neural Information Processing Systems*, 2020.

[8] J. J. Park, P. Florence, J. Straub, R. Newcombe, and S. Lovegrove, "Deepsdf: Learning continuous signed distance functions for shape representation," in *2019 IEEE/CVF Conference on Computer Vision and Pattern Recognition (CVPR)*, 2019, pp. 165–174.

[9] K. Genova, F. Cole, A. Sud, A. Sarna, and T. Funkhouser, "Local deep implicit functions for 3d shape," in *2020 IEEE/CVF Conference on Computer Vision and Pattern Recognition (CVPR)*, jun 2020, pp. 4856–4865.

[10] M. E. Darvin, B. Magnussen, J. Lademann, and W. Köcher, "Multiple spatially resolved reflection spectroscopy for in vivo determination of carotenoids in human skin and blood," *Laser Physics Letters*, vol. 13, no. 9, p. 095601, aug 2016.

[11] D. P. Kingma and J. Ba, "Adam: A method for stochastic optimization," in *3rd International Conference on Learning Representations, ICLR 2015, San Diego, CA, USA, May 7-9, 2015, Conference Track Proceedings*, Y. Bengio and Y. LeCun, Eds., 2015.

[12] O. Biran and C. V. Cotton, "Explanation and justification in machine learning: A survey," in *IJCAI-17 Workshop on Explainable AI (XAI) Proceedings*, 2017.

International Academy, Research,
and Industry Association (IARIA)
412 Derby Way
Wilmington, DE 19810

ISBN 978-1-7138-7121-7

CURRAN ASSOCIATES INC.
proceedings
.com

Ninth International Conference on Informatics and Assistive Technologies for Health-Care, Medical Support and Wellbeing (HEALTHINFO 2024)

Held at NetWare 2024

Nice, France
3-7 November 2024